Computers
and
Adult Learning

ELISABETH GERVER

Computers and Adult Learning

Open University Press
Milton Keynes

Open University Press
A division of
Open University Educational Enterprises Limited
12 Cofferidge Close
Stony Stratford
Milton Keynes MK11 1BY

First published 1984

British Library Cataloguing in Publication Data

Gerver, Elisabeth
Computers and adult learning.
1. Adult education — Great Britain —
Data processing
I. Title
374.'941'02854 LC5225.D3

ISBN 0–335–10577–7
ISBN 0–335–10423–1 Pbk

Text design by W.A.P.
Cover design by Paul Clark

Typeset by S & S Press, Abingdon, Oxfordshire

Printed in Great Britain by M. & A. Thomson Litho Limited,
East Kilbride, Scotland.

In memory of David

Contents

Acknowledgements

Because there is so little published material on computers and adult learning, in writing this book I have been particularly dependent on the informed and patient help of many people. The errors and misjudgements are all mine. The ideas and information have stemmed from conversations with John Anderson, Neil Barnes, Lawson Brown, Tom Carbery, Ken Eason, Richard Freeman, David Hamilton, Lourens Hoekstra, Mary Kennedy, Patsy McIntosh, Phil Odor, Nigel Paine, John Radcliffe, Ian Randall, Bob Salkeld, Eileen Scanlon, Mike Sharples, John Taylor, David Tinsley and Martin Whyte.

The paucity of published research in this field has also meant that I have often had to consult unpublished material. I am grateful to the BBC for their permission to refer to two Broadcasting Research Special Reports (1981 and 1983), to Morphy (1982), and to Radcliffe (1983a); and to Control Data for permission to cite their report for the Home Office on the use of PLATO in Aylesbury Prison.

The book had its philosophical and practical origins in the Scottish Community Education Microelectronics Project, and I should like to thank all those with whom I worked most closely in that project for their sound judgement and practical support. I am especially grateful to Kristen Barrett, James Boyle, Ethel Gray, Tague McFadden, Shiona McDonald, HMI Martyn Roebuck, and David Walker. Above all, I am deeply grateful to HMI Graham Wilson, Chairman of the SCEMP Management Committee, for introducing me to the field and subsequently offering wise counsel.

More generally, I have drawn heavily on the accumulated ideas and experience of colleagues in adult and community education primarily in Scotland but also in the rest of Great Britain and abroad. Here the list is far too long to enumerate, but I should like to record particularly my debt to colleagues in the Scottish Institute of Adult Education and in the Scottish Community Education Council and its predecessor.

For sustained practical help with the book over the academic year in which it was prepared, I am grateful to Queen Margaret College for financing some of the enquiries and for helping with the preparation of much of the illustrative material. Most of all, by agreeing to my year's secondment to SCEMP, the College helped to build the foundations on which the book is laid.

Responsibility for the idea of the book — though not for its imperfect realization — rests with Professor Henry Arthur Jones, who initially encouraged me to believe I could write it, and with John Skelton of the Open University Press, who has tactfully steered me from the first vague ideas to the final completion of the manuscript.

Writing this book has made inordinate demands on my children, Sascha and Miriam, and I hereby apologize for the intrusions it has made into their lives; I am grateful for their tolerance as well as their practical help. In common with many other children today, Sascha is unquestionably better informed about computers than his mother, and has enthusiastically helped me to master my own. Because I have done most of the work at home, using my computer as a word processor, I am also very grateful for the way in which Mrs Ann Sturrock and Mrs Marjory Suttie have protected me from the outside world, housework, and the children where necessary.

The book is dedicated to the memory of my late husband, Dr David Gerver, who was Senior Lecturer in Psychology at the University of Stirling until his death in 1981. His work on simultaneous interpretation and in clinical psychology was deeply committed to improving human communication both creatively and empirically. A similar belief in the possibility of using science and technology to help meet human needs underlies this book. The faith is his, the faults remain my own.

Grateful acknowledgement is made to the following for permission to reproduce their material:

Acorn Computers for the advertisement used in 'The BBC Path towards Computer Literacy'

Control Data for the photographs entitled 'Computers and Training: PLATO in Use'

Sidney Harris for the cartoons entitled 'Sure you can become a systems analyst', 'By putting all our data into code', and 'What it comes down to'

Holt, Rinehart, and Winston for the Garry Trudeau cartoon entitled 'And this is the only other computer . . .'. Copyright © 1982, G. B. Trudeau. Reprinted with permission of Universal Press Syndicate. All rights reserved.

IBM United Kingdom Limited for the advertisement entitled 'My son explained it to me'

Queen Margaret College for the art work used in 'A Taste of Individualised Learning for Adults', 'SCEMP Health Programs', and 'Computer Programs to Serve Diverse Communities'

Scottish Community Education Council for the art work used in 'Adult Educators and Computer Literacy'

Scottish Community Education Microelectronics Project for the program details contained in 'A Taste of Individualised Learning for Adults', 'SCEMP

Health Programs', and 'Computer Programs to Serve Diverse Communities'
Scottish Institute of Adult Education for the cover of the *Scottish Journal of Adult Education* used in 'Adult Educators and Computer Literacy'
University of Dundee Photographic Department for the photograph used in 'Adult Educators and Computer Literacy'

Introduction

To many of those who are concerned with adult education either as providers or as participants, computers and adult learning seem to be incompatible. The idea of computers implies a glamorous, but often alien, branch of high technology, where sophisticated, inaccessible machines are staffed by highly trained and often incomprehensible technicians and programmers. Alternatively, microcomputers tend to be associated with children who are so eager to use them that they will even carry out remedial spelling programs so long as they are rewarded with a game of 'Space Invaders' afterwards. The implications for adult learning are not immediately apparent.

Nor is there an extensive literature on the implications of computers for adult learning. Although there are now a substantial and growing number of books and articles on the uses of computers in schools, reports on developments in computers and adult education are only starting to appear. There are, for instance, no references to the subject in the recent work of Legge (1982). Recently, when I requested the National Institute of Adult Continuing Education to conduct a computer search of recent work in the field, they replied with a total of thirty-four references, many of them to American work of a decade ago. Ironically, while 'an information bomb is exploding around us' (Toffler, 1981), information about computers and adult learning is sparse and fragmented.

It may be, of course, that there is so little information simply because there are so few developments in the field. Is there any evidence that the idea of computers and adult education is more than a fashionable stance? A number of recent developments suggest, tantalizingly, that there may be a growing ferment of activity that has only begun to appear on the surface. To begin with, the Open University has been developing extensive and diverse uses of computers for teaching its adult students, while other universities such as Edinburgh are beginning to express publicly their growing interest in using information technology to open the way to teaching larger numbers of part-time adult students.

There are other indicators too. Using computers to widen adults' access to educational institutions is a major feature of the recently established Educational Counselling and Credit Transfer Information Service. Those who care about the ways in which handicapped adults communicate are showing increasing interest in how computer-based communication aids can make it possible for both physically and mentally handicapped people to participate in education in ways not previously open to them. And in Scotland, the experience since 1981 of the Scottish Community Education Microelectronics Project has confirmed the faith of those who believe that high technology can contribute significantly to adult and community education.

While adult education has not experienced the explosion of interest in computers that has characterized school education, there has been a steady growth of computer applications in adult learning and in access to learning, despite the relative lack of funding for this area by central and local government. At the same time, there has been an unprecedented growth in the ownership of, and presumably interest in, microcomputers both at home and in business. Britain now has a larger proportion of owners of personal computers per head of population than any other country in the world, and as this book goes to press, the enthusiasm for personal computing shows little sign of diminishing.

In adult education this energetic pursuit of personal computer power has resulted in dramatic increases in courses in computing for adults, both for general awareness and in order to learn what can be done with the thing once it's sitting in the living room. The large sales of the books and other materials associated with the popular BBC series *The Computer Programme* and *Making the Most of the Micro* — to say nothing of the sales of the BBC computer itself — also suggest a widespread public fascination with computers.

So, there seem to be several recent developments in computer-based adult learning, and there is overwhelming evidence of public fascination with the subject. But why write a book on the subject? In any case, aren't there already enough books written to introduce people in general and educators in particular to the mysteries of computers? And even granted a need, how will adult educators who are not familiar with computers ever be able to understand all the computer terminology involved?

Let me start with the last question first. This is not a book about computers as such. What Boden (1977) said of her own writing is also true of this book: 'computers are metallic machines of intrinsic interest to electronic engineers but not, as such, to many others. So if you are not enamoured of tin cans, you need not fear to meet any in this book.' The focus lies not on what the machines are and how they have developed, but on what they might offer adult learning. Since my own point of view is that of an adult educator who has become interested in the field rather than someone who is intimate with all the intricacies of computing, the language throughout is that of the non-expert; virtually no technical terms appear.

Secondly, this book is not intended to introduce people to the whole world of computers; some of the many good books which explain computers and their associated information technologies in straightforward terms are noted in Appendix 2. Instead, the book attempts to introduce some of the implications that computers may have for the form and content of adult learning. In order to consider these implications, the book brings together accounts of various recent developments in computer-based adult learning and in related fields such as community education. If, as a result of reading part or all of what follows, those who provide or participate in adult learning feel that they now want to take account of computers, the book will have achieved one of its main purposes.

Next this book takes a fundamentally different approach to computer-based learning than is generally the case. Most published work in the field tends to look first at the phenomenal power of the computer and how it works and then to suggest what it can do for education. I have attempted here instead to ask whether there are any long-standing or particularly intractable problems in adult learning with which computers might provide some help.

Finally, this book differs from many other works on computers and education in the way it explicitly recognises and accepts the many reasons why adults are wary of computers. The problem is not, on the whole, one that exists for those who write about the uses of computers in children's education: most children take to the use of computers with the same fascination and facility that they bring to any fashionable piece of new technology. Adults, however, are less accustomed to innovative ways of learning and are, in any case, rightly uneasy about many of the wider implications of the use of computers.

The book has the purpose and the shape that it does largely as a result of my own experience as project director of the Scottish Community Education Microelectronics Project during 1981 and 1982. SCEMP was initially a three-year project to explore the effective use and potential application of microelectronics in community education. Its major aim was to increase general awareness of the potential scope of microcomputers as a community resource for individualized learning and for providing information.

The project, which was funded by the Scottish Education Department on the advice of the Scottish Council for Community Education, has now been extended until 1987 because it seems to have met such a substantial need in community education in Scotland. In particular, it represents a way of seeing if and how the power of computers can be harnessed to meet the needs of the whole community rather than merely helping those institutions and individuals who can afford to purchase or lease their own computers.

During the course of my work with SCEMP I found that I shared much of the unease that many adult educators feel about the possible use of computers in their work. This unease, it seems to me, is fed by many sources of genuine concern. Most importantly, adult educators and many other people feel alienated from computers for two main reasons: they refuse to be fashionably techno-centred, and they have a sense, often difficult to express publicly, of being baffled by the impenetrable terminology of computer experts.

In this book I have tried therefore to focus on the learning needs of adults rather than on the technical specifications of the equipment that might help to meet some of them. I have also tried to write about computers without using technical terms, although there is a glossary of current jargon in Appendix 1 to link my own accounts with work that is more technically-minded.

Readers who are familiar with computing terminology will probably wince at some of the language, but it seems to me that anyone who writes about computers should do so in language as transparent as possible. The language of computers often seems like Orwell's *Newspeak*, a bastardized code that fails to reflect what most of us know as reality. Moreover, technical language can too readily become a mystifying device to shield those working with computers from informed scrutiny. It may well be that in this attempt to de-mystify computers by using everyday language, I simply annoy both adult educators and computer experts. In that case, I shall at least have succeeded in uniting them in a common cause!

There remain two other important qualifications about the kind of book that this is. It tries to cover some of the more fruitful and more interesting recent developments in computers in adult learning, but it is by no means a comprehensive account of the field. Because of the relative paucity of information about the area there is, no doubt, much interesting work which is not referred to simply because I did not know enough about it; omissions, in other words, signify only my own ignorance, not my belief that any particular development is unimportant.

Secondly, there are certain areas of adult learning which are deliberately omitted because they require specialist treatment of a kind I am in no position to give them: in particular, I have referred only sporadically to the experience of adults who are studying full time in further and higher education, or who are learning in industry, in the armed services and in prisons. Instead, I shall explore several landmarks in the newly discovered territory of computers and adult learning, aware that much remains unaccounted for.

Chapter 1, *Why Computers Matter*, argues that everyone who cares about adult learning needs to take serious account of the possibilities and implications of computers and the associated new technologies of microelectronics and telecommunications. It then speculates about the reasons why many adult educators and, indeed, many adults in general, have so far been sceptical about the advantages of computers as a learning tool and wary of coming into closer contact with them.

Chapter 2, *The Character of Computers*, considers first the ways in which computers are often represented in the books and films that help to shape our sense of reality. It then discusses at some length major doubts and fears about the increasingly widespread use of computers, particularly the ways in which, depending on the context in which they are introduced and the purposes of using them, computers can be a powerful enabler of political and social evil. Finally, this chapter briefly outlines the main characteristics of contemporary computers, emphasizing their power, utility and relative ease of operating.

These first chapters set the context. Chapter 3, *Learning with Computers*, considers what computers might actually have to offer to adult learning. It looks first at some current and long-standing difficulties in adult education and asks whether computers might provide part of an answer to alleviating certain problems. This discussion is followed by an examination of some of the ways in which computers are now being used in adult education, and a number of actual programs are described as illustrations of what is being and might be done in this field. Finally, the chapter looks at the difficulties and implications of using computers for adult learning.

Chapter 4, *Learning about Computers*, tries to make a case for computer literacy and examines what may be involved in such a concept. It also looks at possible ways of educating adults about computers, and tries to analyse the reasons for the apparent success or failure of different approaches.

Chapter 5, *Computers and Community Education*, considers the wider problem of how one might most effectively use computers to meet more general needs for certain kinds of information in the community as a whole. It proposes a number of potential uses for computers in community groups and considers the impact already made by computers in certain voluntary organizations. Finally, it outlines a number of factors to consider in deciding whether to computerize administrative or information services within community organizations.

The last chapter (6) *Computers for All?*, speculates about the implications of the growing use of computers for the future shape of adult learning. One of the concerns here is the way in which the development of computers so far has tended largely to exclude women, who have traditionally formed the largest group of participants in adult education. Overall, this chapter considers practical ways in which adult educators might harness the power of computers for their own work now. It also looks ahead to the kind of choices about learning that both individuals and professional adult educators may have to make in the future as a consequence of developments in computers and allied technologies.

The Appendices provide first a glossary of terms that are often encountered in the literature of computers and education, and then a few suggestions about where to go for further information and advice about the possibilities of using computers in adult learning.

1

Why Computers Matter

Information technology deepens all our choices.

(Shirley Williams, 1982)

Because of their powerful potential and their equally impressive limitations the new information technologies, dominated by developments in computers, may deepen our choices but may also leave us less confident about making choices based on any real understanding of the implications of computerizing our society. Some of our unease is inherent in the very nature of computers both in reality and as part of our fantasies; these characteristics form the subject of Chapter 2.

For adult educators in particular, there are more possibilities for adult learning and therefore more difficult and deeper choices than ever before. As I shall argue in Chapter 2, many of these choices are shaped by the ways in which computers are already affecting our lives. It therefore follows that where they care about responding to social change, adult educators will have to take account of computers and their implications. In the present chapter I shall suggest that there are also directly educational reasons why computers matter to those of us who care about adult learning.

The Pluralism of Adult Learning

Because this book is not intended to be a rigorous academic study of the barely emerging field of computers and adult learning, I shall not engage in the usual practice of careful definition of terms. The nearest I shall come to a definition of *computer* is in Chapter 2. In the meantime I should like to extract myself from the terminological quagmire of what is meant by such terms as *adult education*, *recurrent education*, *continuing education*, and *lifelong learning* by merely noting a few examples of what I mean by the term *adult learning*.

Like Kidd (1973), I believe that 'there is no answer to the question, "What is learning", any more than there is to, "What is electricity" '. The characteristics of adult learning are multiple and inter-related, although they all seem to share a process of discovering something new. There are several other characteristics which one could reasonably suppose that all adults bring to their experience as learners. They will, for instance, usually be voluntary learners and therefore, at least initially, highly motivated to learn. Because they have usually chosen to learn, they will tend to have high expectations of the value and the sheer delight of learning. They will also have acquired certain characteristic, individual ways of responding to experience, so that any group of say, middle-aged adults will be more varied in its expectations, its responses and therefore its learning styles than any comparable group of children. They will probably also have many competing demands on their time and their emotional and physical energy, and will thus often be intolerant of any educational demands which they do not see as essential to what they want to learn. They may also be sensitive to the social context of their learning and especially vulnerable to a fear of failing in public. In other words, they will often be simultaneously ruthless and vulnerable.

Obviously, these characteristics of adult learners will appear in varying degrees in any individual, depending on his or her particular circumstances. Those who perceive themselves as having failed at school and who have taken little part in educational activity since then will often be particularly vulnerable to the fear of failing yet again. Professionals who are re-training may have to be particularly ruthless about the amount of time and attention that they can afford to give to learning. Women returning to formal education after spending years at home caring for dependents may sometimes be so lacking in self-confidence that they place the demands of their own educational experience lowest on a long list of time-consuming priorities. Older people may feel most powerfully the need to relate their present learning to their past experience. In each of these cases, the characteristics of adult learning are present, but they differ in their preponderance.

The contexts in which adults learn are also highly varied, and more and more often people are shifting from one context or mode of learning to another. The contexts range from those which Tough (1971) characterized as 'learning projects', where adults informally plan and carry out deliberate attempts to improve their knowledge or skills, to various enforced environments in which adults may learn involuntarily, such as mental institutions or prisons.

I am concerned here primarily, however, with those situations in which adults take part in learning programmes which have been deliberately designed for them rather than for children. I shall include formal as well as non-formal, and community learning at all levels when it is undertaken voluntarily by adults who have experienced a break from full-time education.

This book will include, therefore, the learning that takes place in higher and further education where adults participate as 'mature students', as well as the forms of learning traditionally seen as the foundation of adult education — those provided by the local authorities, the university extra-mural departments, and voluntary agencies such as the Workers Educational Association and community organizations.

The book will also take account of some of the contexts within which adults undertake open learning or learning at a distance, such as the mass media, the correspondence colleges, and libraries. The kind of training for specific vocational or professional purposes that is increasingly dominating the lives of many people both in and out of work will also be considered; however, the field of computer-based training is a major area of development in its own right (see Dean and Whitlock, 1983), and I shall not try to cover it extensively.

Because adult learning seems to be such a pluralistic phenomenon, the possible contributions that computers might make to the field are diverse and uneven. In certain areas such as training, computer-based methods are being increasingly widely applied; in other areas, such as evening classes in general education for adults, the use of a computer for direct teaching purposes is rare. Moreover, as Chapter 2 will indicate, most contemporary developments in computers tend to be highly specific rather than general in their applications. In what follows, therefore, I shall often note particular areas in which computers might be helpful in adult learning without intending to make more general statements about their possible overall value. Discussion of the wider issues will take place in Chapter 6.

Adults and Computers: the Educational Potential

Do computers offer any real potential to the adult educator? At first glance there are a number of intriguing possibilities. Some of the characteristics of adult learning appear to dovetail remarkably well with certain facilities offered by computers. For instance, the computer can take account of the individual differences among students in ways that are simply not possible for say, a single tutor teaching a group of twenty people. Students using computers for learning can progress at their own speed, and the computer will remain a patient, untiring tutor, who moreover will not announce any failure in public in the way that a misjudged reply to a question in a class might do.

The sheer variety of choices and possible outcomes available through using computers may also mean that individual adults can reach for their own goals in learning rather than feeling constrained by the needs of other learners in a group. As a powerful and versatile form of educational technology, too, the computer can offer new and often imaginative forms of learning that can be a delight in themselves. Computer simulations can allow students to experiment with situations that would otherwise be too remote, complicated or dangerous. And when it is used to assess progress, the computer can provide instant responses in a way simply not possible for a hard-pressed tutor with many other commitments as well. Time, too, is at a premium for many adult students, and there is a growing body of literature that suggests that at least certain kinds of learning may be accomplished more quickly by way of a computer than by more traditional methods. For physically handicapped adults, computers offer the possibility of being able to communicate, and so of being able to learn, in ways which had previously been closed to them.

But do adults actually like using computers as a tool for their own learning? As yet there is insufficient evidence to form any sound conclusion, but there are a number of indications that using computers may be a popular means of learning, at least for certain adults. In Scotland, for instance, evaluation of the popular 'Computers for All' exhibitions of computer programs for community education suggested that 'adults . . . seemed to be more willing than children to be educated . . . by the computer programs' (Barrett, 1982). Similarly, Ross (1980) refers to a 'blossoming popularity of computer-assisted instruction amongst students'. The fact that a number of agencies in adult education are now examining the possibilities of computers in their own work, as discussed later in this chapter, is further evidence that at least some adult educators believe that computers may be a popular mode of learning.

Indeed, the possible fit between the characteristics of adult learning and of computers seems so good that one commentator has asserted that computer-based learning 'is inherently compatible with adult learners. . . . It provides a very close match with what we know about adults in learning situations' (Reynolds, 1983). Clearly, this apparent compatibility warrants attention from adult educators.

But there are other important reasons too why computers should matter to anyone concerned with adult learning. It is well recognized that certain learning needs of adults are inadequately met by conventional methods; here again computers seem to present attractive options. For instance, many studies on the relationship between adult learning and social class comment that men of the lower socio-economic groups rarely seem to participate in adult education (ACACE, 1982a). Experience with computers in community education suggests that just these groups may be attracted to using computers and may even participate in educational experiences that they would not have undertaken in more traditional ways.

Another pressing need often felt by those concerned with adult learning is the establishment of a comprehensive adult educational advisory service that could help current and future learners to discover what opportunities are available to suit their own particular circumstances. Here too, computers offer attractive steps towards a solution. Indeed, the national Educational Counselling and Credit Transfer Information Service currently being established is already taking advantage of the opportunities offered by computers for providing educational information and thereby widening access to formal education for adults. Because the service will be computerized, its information officers will be able to offer 'information to help match individual needs to available courses leading to recognized qualifications' (ECCTIS, 1983).

The administrative help that can be provided to adult education by computers is not limited to such information. Providers of adult education are increasingly attracted to the possibilities of easing their own administrative loads by computerizing many of their more time-consuming functions such as time-tabling, up-dating information leaflets, maintaining financial records, and so on.

Computers offer tempting personal help to adult educators too, especially for word processing of reports, articles, texts and even books. This book, for instance, is being prepared on a computer that allows me to type in all the words, correct the many errors, change passages as I choose, and finally print out a copy good enough to send to the publisher without having to type a final fair copy. Indeed, for amateur typists such as myself (and presumably many others too), word processing represents a new freedom, ease and speed of communicating.

Further afield, computer systems linked to one another by telecommunications offer even more enticing educational and educative possibilities. One can already search for many different kinds of information by way of computers, and many previously tedious tasks of locating books, finding relatively obscure information and so on are now comparatively simple to carry out by means of computers linked to one another.

However, as I shall discuss later in this chapter, there are certain fundamental limitations to what the computer can reasonably be said to offer to adult learning. The most characteristic feature of computers is that they can enhance our ability to acquire and to manipulate information, especially when they are linked with telecommunications. However, as Scriven (1981) reminds us, 'information is not education'. It may be, then, that some of the apparent potential of computers in adult learning will be less realizable and less relevant than it seemed at first. But in the areas noted above there is ample evidence that adult learners and those who provide for them at least need to consider the feast of possibilities for using computers in learning.

In addition to the educational and educative possibilities of computers in adult learning, there are other important reasons why computers matter to adult educators. In the first place, the sheer growth in public and private use of computers demands a comparable awareness and response from adult education.

The Ubiquitous Computer

In Britain today, even people who prefer not to make any personal use of computers find that many of the ordinary transactions of their lives are increasingly affected by computer applications. In our financial lives, most of our bills from large organizations now come in computerized form, and we are becoming accustomed to withdrawing money from our bank accounts by computer-linked cash dispensers. Most of our dealings with government departments depend on computerized records of information.

When we go to the cinema, we are more and more likely to encounter computers and their programs as major characters in films, as with HAL in *2001* or JOSHUA in *War Games*; computers, too, play a crucial role in the action of films such as *Rollover*, where a turning point in the story depends on the central character fraudulently extracting information from the central computer records of a major bank.

We are all aware, too, of the impersonal, chilling and ubiquitous presence of computers in the preparations for nuclear war that shadow all our lives. Here, as in the other instances I have already mentioned, we are aware of the presence of computers but are often uneasy or even passionately concerned about the potential for control and for manipulation of our lives that computers can provide. These matters are discussed at some length in Chapter 2. In this chapter, I shall present a snapshot of a world that is, whether we personally choose it to be so or not, increasingly dominated by computer applications. This fact in itself demands the serious attention of anyone who is concerned with helping adults better to understand and to cope with the realities of our world.

Computers are also becoming increasingly important to people in their personal lives. More and more people own computers: in 1982, over one million personal computers were bought in Britain (Allason, 1983), many of them for children, who have an infallible eye for things that look impressive but are easy to manage. There are now personal computers in 7 per cent of British homes, and this figure is expected to increase to 22 per cent by 1988 (Smith, K., 1983). And there has been an accompanying growth in information about computing, ranging from computer clubs for enthusiasts to magazines about personal computers for the general public; even in a village like my own the local newsagent carries a good supply of computer magazines.

Learning about Computers

The second main reason why computers should be of serious interest to adult educators is the substantial and growing demand for learning about computers. Probably the most publicized of recent attempts to help adults to learn about computers is the BBC's Computer Literacy Project, in which strikingly large numbers of learners have participated. About seven million adults saw some part of *The Computer Programme* on television, and this figure increased to about nine million for the follow-up programme, *Making the Most of the Micro* (Radcliffe and Salkeld, 1983).

An introductory course on computer programming, presented by the National Extension College as an integral part of the BBC project, had sold about 120,000 copies by the middle of 1983 (Freeman, 1983), while *The Computer Book*, published by the BBC as an introduction to computers for non-experts, sold during part of 1982 'at a level more usually associated with popular best-selling novels' (Radcliffe and Salkeld, 1983). The Computer Referral Service, which provides information about the project and puts people in touch with local opportunities to learn about computers, had received nearly 200,000 enquiries by the middle of 1983 (ibid). Demand for the accompanying micro computer exceeded all expectation, and by mid

1983 over 150,000 BBC Computers had been sold (ibid).

At the level of formal computer courses in adult education there has been a dramatic increase over the past few years. Radcliffe's (1983b) laconic comment that 'classes and courses generally seem to have been well-subscribed' is an understatement; many providers of courses linked to the BBC Computer Literacy Project reported that their classes were over-subscribed two and three times over (Salkeld, 1983).

A similar pattern of enthusiasm for computing amongst adult learners emerges from a comparison between the numbers of courses in mathematics and computing offered to adults in British universities in 1980/81 and 1981/82. In the former year, 200 courses in mathematics and computing were offered; by the following year this figure had increased to 318 (Taylor, 1983). Local authority provision seems to show a comparable increase: in Leeds in 1981, for instance, eleven introductory computing evening classes were offered; by 1982 this figure doubled to twenty-one (Banks, 1983).

The rapid growth of books about computers for the general public has also been striking. The usual approach of these books, called by titles that make computers seem both powerful and homely, such as *The Electronic Cottage* (Deken, 1981) is to take a leap into the projected electronic future with its exciting, if often specious, promises of more of everything for everybody and then to focus more specifically on what people can do with the computers they have bought in the meantime.

At the same time there is a growing collection of books which try seriously to examine the social implications of the computerized society; a number of these are referred to in Appendix 2. A glance at the current prospectuses of the BBC and the independent broadcasters also shows their continuing and increasing provision of programmes dealing with computers. The evident existence of a substantial and growing audience for such books and programmes, combined with massive popular enthusiasm for computing at many levels, strongly suggests that this is a field of enormous potential for adult educators.

Children and Computers

The third reason why computers clamour for the attention of adult educators is the clear need to help adults to come to terms with the extraordinary communion between children and computers. Anything that can be said about adults' awareness and experience of computers is overwhelmed by an avalanche of evidence of children's involvement with them. Anyone who has ever taken part in a public exhibition of computers will know that the desire of children to use the computers will almost swamp any other aims the exhibitors may have had in mind, while the clusters of children around computers in shops are a familiar phenomena.

Where adult courses in computing have nearly doubled over the past two years, computer camps for children have multiplied perhaps a hundred fold (Levi, 1983). Commercially, advertisements for home computers stress the ways in which children will immediately take to them with delight, and the programs available for such computers seem to be directed primarily at children, especially in the focus on computer games. Indeed, advertisements increasingly assume that parents will be introduced to computers by their children.

"Sure you can become a systems analyst if you want to — but tell Daddy, What is a systems analyst?"

The extraordinary extent and rapidity of the development of computer familiarity amongst children in Britain has been enhanced by the promotion of computer use in schools, particularly through the two major agencies in the field, the Microelectronics Education Programme and the Scottish Microelectronics Development Programme, and by government promotion and support of purchases of computer systems by both primary and secondary schools. In many cases, however, as teachers already know to their despair, children's familiarity and competence with computers far exceeds any formal provision for them at school.

Such widespread computer literacy amongst children clearly raises a need for their parents to feel equally at home with the new information technologies. The need to help adults to feel at home with computers, however, is not a pressing concern amongst the commercial providers. A representative from IBM (the major computer manufacturer) commented recently that 'with children and young adults adapting so easily, eventually the problem of educating mid-life adults in first-time computer use will cease to exist' (Lean, 1983).

Nor has the need to help adults to come to terms with computers been felt significantly at the level of central government. With the exception of the Scottish Community Education Microelectronics Project, money from central government has not been spent on adult computer literacy. Even in SCEMP the budget is miniscule compared with the overall sums currently being devoted to promoting the uses of computers in schools.

Some local authorities do feel a serious obligation to help parents to bridge the generation gap between their children's computer literacy and their own comparative illiteracy: in Fife, for instance, the 'Education Authority is sensitive to the increasing need for computer literacy amongst parents whose children are being introduced to the new technology in the schools' (McDonald, 1983a). Overall, however, it seems that although current promotion of new information technologies in schools and formal further and higher education will continue and probably even intensify, there is unlikely to be significant stimulus from central government for encouraging and supporting the development of computer literacy for adults.

Despite the relative lack of interest — or at least of funding — by government in the field of computers and adult learning, 'the need for some kind of facility through which people can gain access to information and advice about computers and computing exists . . . and will continue at all levels' (Morphy, 1982). The full case for the need for adult computer literacy will be made in Chapter 4. But for the moment it is sufficient to acknowledge that — if only to meet their children on more equal terms — adults have a pressing need for computer literacy.

Current Developments in Computers and Adult Learning

Finally, computers matter to adult educators because they are already being used to support adult learning in a number of significant areas. At the level of higher education for adults, the Open University has necessarily had to develop computerized records and administrative services because of the sheer numbers with which it has had to cope. It has also made interesting use of computers for tutorials and for simulations, especially in its science, technology and mathematics courses but also more recently in social sciences and the arts. At present a number of course teams in the Open University are planning computer components as an integral element in their courses (Lockwood and Cooper, 1980).

At the opposite end of the spectrum in community education, computers are also becoming increasingly important both for administration and for adult learning. Here the picture has been coloured by the presence of the Scottish Community Education Microelectronics Project, which might be seen perhaps as artificially cultivating the use of computers in adult learning in a kind of educational hot-house. It is notable, however, that where SCEMP has lent computers to organizations in community education to experiment with, virtually all of the bodies concerned have decided to acquire their own computers once the loan had come to an end (SCEMP, 1983). The sheer volume of enquiries to SCEMP also suggests a high degree of interest from both field workers and those to whom they are responsible (ibid. and SCEMP, 1982a).

The creation of computer programs specifically for adults has also been thriving: despite the difficulties of development, SCEMP by the middle of 1983 had developed more than twenty programs for community education (SCEMP, 1983). Particularly in the areas of adult basic education and of health education, computer programs for adults are being increasingly developed, as may be seen in Chapter 3.

Indeed, the use of computers in community education is now increasing at so rapid a rate in Britain that since 1982 a newsletter, 'Community Computing Network', has been published to link all the groups who are developing applications for computers in their communities (see Appendix 2 for further details). By mid 1983, there were already over eighty organizations and individuals in Britain who regularly received this newsletter.

Finally, there seems to be a substantial amount of interest by some adult educators in the field of computers and adult learning. The topic has appeared at international conferences of adult educators, and there were a number of national meetings, many of them over-subscribed, on the subject in Britain during 1982 and 1983.

The use of computers in adult learning is also starting to appear as a subject in the professional journals of adult education (see, for instance, Banks, 1983 and Wilson, 1983). The fact that in 1983 enquiries to SCEMP, which started in 1981, were still running at between ten and fifteen a week in a country as small as Scotland also suggests that in the field of computers and adult learning it is 'as if the lid had been lifted off a pot that one supposed to have been full of cool water and discovered suddenly that it was already simmering' (SCEMP, 1982a).

Government policy being what it is, at least as this book goes to press, this interest in using computers in adult education is likely to increase rather than diminish. In their specific proposals as well as in their more general promotion of the new information technologies, government departments and agencies are dramatically increasing computer applications that have direct implications for adult learning. In the future, for instance, the government's Alvey project, set up to fund research into advanced computers, is 'likely to concentrate on fundamentals like the way people work and the best way for that work to be done with computers' (Lamb, 1983). Recently, the Information Technology initiative and its successors have been important attempts to educate people to the supposed benefits of using computers and associated telecommunications and microelectronics.

In publications by government agencies, too, there are increasing numbers of references to the advantages offered using computers for learning; the

MSC's 'Towards an Adult Training Strategy' (1983), for example, refers throughout to the possibilities of using the new technologies in adult training. There will also be a longer term cumulative effect of the current policy of energetically promoting the educational and administrative applications of computers in schools.

Finally, in the world of formal education for adults, the many new appointments in information technology in colleges and universities from 1982–83 onwards will also affect directly or indirectly those adults who return to study as mature students. The Council for National Academic Awards (1982) has already advised all the institutions which it supports to consider the significance of information technology for their present and future courses. The same process of evaluation is taking place at university level, where the major area for government-financed expansion appears to lie in the new information technologies. Indeed, the whole field of information technology is rapidly becoming a discipline and a subject of academic enquiry in its own right.

The growing emphasis being placed on open or distance learning in many institutions will also undoubtedly result in further exploitations of using computers for adult learning. The growth of courses in open or distance learning has been one of the major phenomena of adult learning in the past few years; in Scotland, for instance, the number of such courses on offer in 1981 was only 47, but by 1983 it had reached 190 (SCET, 1983). In England and Wales the many programmes offered by correspondence and flexi-study have also grown enormously over the past few years. Throughout Britain, as Chapter 3 will illustrate, such courses in open or distance learning for adults are making increasing use of computers.

Yet, despite this evidence of the increasing importance of computers for adult learning, many adult educators remain at best sceptical of the feasibility and benefits of using computers. As Chapter 2 will consider, there are many sound reasons why all of us may be doubtful and indeed fearful about the consequences of computerizing our society. But there are also good reasons for a particular scepticism about using computers for adult learning, and I shall now turn to the educational reasons why many adult educators may be wary of computers.

Computers Against Adult Learning

The two major reasons for the current widespread scepticism about the advantages of using computers in adult learning seem to be that computerized education often appears to distort the nature of adult learning fundamentally, and that there is a plethora of practical obstacles in the way of using computers in adult education. As the rest of this book argues, neither of these reasons is sufficient justification for rejecting the use of computers in adult learning. But the reasons themselves merit further examination.

Many adult educators sense a radical discordance between what com-

"By putting all our data into code, our competitors can't read it, our unauthorized personnel can't read it, and I'm afraid, neither can we."

puters offer and the aims of adult learning. This sense of a fundamentally different approach in each field was expressed by Malcolm Knowles (1983) in an account of the 'year of high anticipations and repeated frustrations' that he spent after acquiring a personal computer. He found, for instance, that the computer manual

> violates many principles of adult learning; it is very pedagogical: (1) It makes me memorize commands by rote memory without my understanding how I would use them in writing letters, articles and books; (2) It makes me practise the commands by playing games, which I am not interested in. Furthermore, my confidence is shaken constantly when I follow the instructions in the manual or on the screen and the computer does not do what the instructions say it will.

My personal experience of using a variety of computers confirms the experience of Knowles. In each case I have tried to master the manual about how to operate the machine, and in each case I have been so foiled that I have resorted to asking someone more knowledgeable what I should do in order to get the machine to carry out a particular function. So the way in which manufacturers present their machines to the general public does not inspire confidence in the ability of computers to support adult learning.

But this difficulty is merely one symptom of a more general problem about the ways in which computers tend to interact with people. The overall issue is, of course, that

> the human being is the dialectical opposite of the machine in that he [sic] is slow, inconsistent, unreliable but highly creative, whereas the machine is fast, consistent and reliable but totally uncreative' (Cooley, 1980).

Even given this fundamental mismatch between people and computers, many adult educators are entirely justified in mistrusting the public face of computers. In the first place, the massive high-pressured market for computers has ensured that the major criteria for successful selling of computers is not whether they can answer real human needs but rather whether people can be persuaded to buy them. Indeed, as one writer recently put it in a computer magazine, 'were it not for the myths and fantasies home computers would not sell to anyone who wasn't an enthusiast' (Burton, 1983). The myths, however, live on: 'the adverts tell you you can do anything with a computer, you ought to have one, it'll solve all your problems' (ibid).

The problem of mismatch between what the world of computers promises and the purposes for which human beings want to use it has now become so acute that entire books are devoted to the subject (see, for instance, Covvey and McAlister, 1982). Increasingly, writers on the subject stress that 'it will not be . . . worthwhile having a computer in the home (or in business for that matter) until its limitations are widely acknowledged' (Burton, 1983). Yet the phenomenon of what has been termed 'conspicuous computing' (Covvey and McAlister, 1982) continues to be promoted enthusiastically in the world of computers: at home, in business and in education. In wanting to avoid the purchase of computers that might lie as underused as they currently do in at least some homes and schools, adult educators are merely being realistically cautious.

There are other facets of the unwillingness of many adult educators to become involved with computers. Many educators — and I have been one of them — have tried to learn about computers only to be faced by two equally repellent barriers. First, many so-called introductions to computers start from the premise that it is the machines that matter above all. A recent book about new information technology in education, for instance, revealingly asks: 'Which are the devices and systems that belong to new information technology? What can we do with each?' (Hawkridge, 1983a) . Another recent commentator suggests that 'the computer offers new possibilities in terms of educational practice; in some sense we should be seeking a "problem to fit the solution" ' (Skues, 1983). The stance is by no means confined to educational technologists. Generally, in the field of computer technology, there is 'a mode of thought that has become altogether too traditional: . . . it begins with a great many solutions and then looks for problems' (Weizenbaum, 1979).

This emphasis on the machine rather than on human needs often stands between adult educators and computers. I have attended a number of seminars for novices in which the major part of the session consisted of detailed description and analysis of machines rather than discussion of those purposes for which they might be seriously used. Conversations with computer users often take the form of quoting the specifications of the machines before anyone discusses what they are good for and, indeed, this latter topic is sometimes omitted altogether. Of this focus on machines, adult educators are rightly dismissive.

A second barrier that can confront anyone who wants to learn about computers as a novice is that the language used about the topic is often impenetrable as well as at times de-humanizing. Thus, one has to learn about hardware, software and even liveware, instead of machines, programs and people. The language of computers has sometimes fruitfully enlarged our own language and our ideas of what can be done: the idea of 'networking' (linking machines over distances), for instance, can significantly enlarge our ways of thinking about forms of adult learning. But for most adult educators, the effect of computer jargon has been to cut them off from the world of computers, making even simple processes seem mysterious and incomprehensible because of the language in which they are described.

The language of computers often alienates adult educators because it seems to be solely that of instrumental reason. Its thrust is almost entirely functional: as one computer commentator put it, if our generation is defined as living in the age of information technology, then 'our speciality is not wisdom or . . . thinking. Our speciality is organizing power' (Scarrot, 1981). The language used within this context not surprisingly often sounds like an aggressive parody of technical jargon, with words such as RAM, bug, byte, and menu-driven. Even linguistically, then, it is not a world in which most adult educators would choose to live.

As well as these barriers to computers, adult educators will often be suspicious of a world from which women are almost entirely excluded. The question as to why computing should be a male preserve and what might be done about it is considered throughout the book. There is extensive and overwhelming evidence of this phenomenon, and for now I shall merely note a few indicators of the trend as it touches on adult learning.

The dominant feature of any public exhibition of computers is that it will be overwhelmed by young males. In its first year the Scottish Commmunity Education Microelectronics Project found most of its support in local communities from male workers, and most of its voluntary programming was carried by men. The BBC, too, have noted a pronounced male preponderance in those providing and those taking courses in computing as part of the Computer Literacy Project (Salkeld, 1983) although, in a striking exception to the rule, the numbers of male and female viewers of the original programmes in the project were nearly evenly balanced (Radcliffe and Salkeld, 1983).

More generally, providers of computing for adults at all levels tend to be male themselves and to assume that their audiences will be so too; thus, for instance, the Open University's 'Micros in Schools' brochure for school teachers contains pictures of nineteen male figures in all, with only two women (both of whom are merely observing use of the computers rather than actually engaging with them).

Much the same imbalance is observed in the computer magazines directed at enthusiasts, where the representation of male to female is roughly ten to one. The bias, then, is not confined to computers in education but appears to be more generally true of computing as a whole. As Weizenbaum (1976) has noticed, there are no women amongst the fraternity of the 'compulsive programmers'; similarly, the 'computer widower' is unknown, although 'computer widows' are a common occurence. It is not fortuitous that over 90 per cent of purchasers of the popular BBC Computer have been men (BBC, 1983).

Traditionally, however, the world of adult education has a high proportion of women, in formal and informal learning as learners and as tutors. For many adult learners and educators the male world of computers will therefore seem particularly alien. This bias of computers as a male preserve both makes it difficult for those women who would like to enter it and 'holds the seeds of a long-term problem' (Hawkridge, 1983a).

As well as acknowledging these broader reservations about the role of computers in adult learning, one may also wonder about the educational wisdom of using computers with adults. Young adults and children learn to use computers with comparative ease and sometimes with astonishing rapidity and facility. Older adults, however, 'may have a deep-seated fear of computers in general, and a strong resistance to the abstract nature of computer-based learning in particular' (Lean, 1983). The reservations that adults often feel about using computers for learning are also demonstrated in the relatively low take-up of computer-assisted learning in certain Open University courses where it is offered: the take-up ranges from 15 to 40 per cent (Jones and Scanlon, 1981). Even those students who did use them had a realistic impression of the potential and actual difficulties associated with their use (ibid).

A further major obstacle in the way of making more extensive use of computers in adult learning appears in the suspect educational characteristics of many of the computer programs so far developed. One problem is that so few programs of potential value to adult learning have yet been developed. Indeed, in the field of computers and learning generally, there are not yet many fully developed programs of probable educational value. Speaking of the major advances in educational technology, including computers, over the past ten years, one researcher comments that 'most are still under development, their possible contributions to education unknown' (Sharples, 1982a).

As another leading exponent of information technology has said, the questions are 'what information technology can do that human teachers cannot, and whether information technology can teach any better? . . . These questions cannot yet be answered with confidence' (Hawkridge, 1983b).

One reason why the questions cannot yet be answered is that there has been virtually no serious evaluation carried out in the field of the use of computers in adult learning and very little even in child learning. As Chapter 3 discusses further, the field cries out for evaluation that has not yet taken place, although there have been several preliminary investigations.

Meanwhile, many of the programs currently being displayed in education have serious disadvantages for adult learning. Some of them are so child centred that adults would hesitate to use them for serious purposes. Others tend to conform slavishly, if colourfully, to a model of mechanistic programmed learning that merely uses a computer screen in place of a programmed text. Programs of both sorts (and more than a few combine the two) are considered in Chapter 3, but adult educators are rightly wary of using them.

A further difficulty about adults using the kinds of programs that currently exist for children occurs because of the specificity of good computer programs, which may be impressively helpful and successful in highly limited contexts but which cannot easily be transferred from one learning milieu or syllabus to another. An analogous difficulty arises with any attempt to use North American programs in Britain: one American health-education program used in Scotland, for instance, assumed that its users know their levels of cholesterol and blood pressure as readily as their age and height.

Some of these ways in which computers may seem to be programmed against adult learning limit their possible uses by adult educators quite fundamentally. Others, as Chapter 3 and 6 will consider, are comparatively minor problems which in some cases have already been successfully tackled. But there are also other kinds of computer problems that may confront adult educators — those arising from the practical difficulties of using today's computers. While virtually all of these problems can be solved by sufficient care and imagination, they still need to be recognized.

Computers in the Real World

Perhaps the most common, if often unexpressed, reaction to actually using computers is a feeling that there is an uneasy mismatch between what the machines should do and what they actually perform. The facts of machine failure, and the sometimes disastrous consequences of it, are too often glossed over. First, some anecdotal evidence. Several months ago I had to write an extended article about computers in a particularly short time, and planned to use my new computer to do so, as its word processing capabilities would cut the preparation time by at least half. The computer, however, broke down almost as soon as I had begun; the supplier was a considerable distance away; and I was left to find twice the time to do the work on an ordinary typewriter.

Throughout the first year's experience in the Scottish Community Education Microelectronics Project all of us had to make frequent allowances for the possible breakdown of machines and for the ways in which people might abuse them. One of the machines involved needed a key to run it, but the key was shared with another user and was therefore rarely available at the very time the machine was needed.

In most objective reports on computer applications, the rate of technical failure at one level or another is remarkably consistent, running at about 25 per cent or more. On receiving their BBC Computers 27 per cent of the customers found that the machines themselves were defective (BBC, 1983). Over 20 per cent of those replying to a questionnaire about their use of a computer-based information system in the project 'Prestel for People' felt that the equipment had not been reliable (Kania, 1983). During the trial run of a computer-assisted training scheme at a college in Canada, there was a complete failure of the system on 30 per cent of the days involved (Loyer, 1983). Other instances abound (see, for instance, Covvey and McAlister, 1982), even if there is often a considerable amount of pressure not to report them.

I have not cited these accounts merely to draw attention to the truism that all machines are fallible. We all accept that our cars or our televisions or our washing machines will occasionally be out of order. But computer failure appears to be so embarrassing to those who work with computers that information about it is often sparse or even suppressed. Yet it remains a factor that anyone who is considering the possible use of computers has to acknowledge so that work for which computers are used is safeguarded as far as possible.

A second striking feature of contemporary computers is that they are very likely to consist of many different kinds of equipment, only some of which will be compatible with others. Some of the incompatibility is linguistic: the language BASIC, which is the most commonly used language in microcomputers, has many different dialects, each of which is incompatible with the others, while the language as a whole is incompatible with other computer languages.

The different parts of computer systems made by different manufacturers also tend to be incompatible with one another. The ways of using each computer also differ from one machine to another: learning to use a large computer attached to a major educational institution might be little help in coming to terms with the kind of machine one might use for an evening class or at home. Here again, as with the problem of machine failure, the difficulty is surmountable, but the hyperbolic language that often accompanies advertisements for computers might well lead a newcomer to ignore the possible dangers.

The adult educator who nevertheless wants to investigate the possibility of using computers in his work will also be faced with the tricky questions of the expense of investing in the equipment itself and the much greater trouble or expense of acquiring suitable educational programs for adults. The expense of the equipment in itself is probably no absolute barrier, as the cost continues to decrease dramatically while the capacity of computers continues to rise. The question of creating or buying suitable programs, however, is a far more serious obstacle and will be discussed at some length in Chapters 3 and 6, which will offer possible solutions. Meanwhile, this particular problem will become more tractable as more and more adult educators become familiar with computers.

All of these reservations about the wisdom and feasibility of using computers in adult learning are based on the fundamental caution of not expecting computers to do more than can reasonably be asked of them. The kinds of things that adult educators might well want to ask them to do are discussed in Chapters 3, 4 and 5, with speculations about future possibllities and developments in Chapter 6. But we can consider these matters in more detail, we need to look more closely at some of the things that are now happening as men and women try to come to terms with computers, whether by choice or necessity. How people perceive and interact with computers therefore forms the subject of Chapter 2.

2

The Character of Computers

The computer is the Proteus of machines.

(Seymour Papert, 1980)

There are many senses in which one may agree with Papert's vision of the computer as Proteus. This Greek mythological figure is now primarily associated with the idea of versatility and changeability from his power of assuming whatever shape he pleased. Much the same is true of contemporary computers, which can assume very different characteristics and have different capabilities depending on their context and purpose.

But the characterization of the computer as Proteus is also appropriate because of his association with knowledge and information: just as the Greek figure knew all things — past, present and future — so the computer is often described as 'by far the most powerful tool that man [sic] has ever had for handling information of all kinds' (Laver, 1980). And just as Proteus disliked telling what he knew and had to be captured and held fast before giving an answer, so also many computers seem to be unwilling to yield their information until they are queried by experts who can overcome the apparent barriers.

For other reasons as well, the metaphorical representation of the computer as a Greek mythological figure is particularly apt. In the world of computer programs and applications, Greek references abound: thus, one can learn with PLATO, the computer-based training system distributed by Control Data; one can consult ORACLE, the computer-based public information system offered by independent television; children can explore the nature of knowledge with LOGO, the computer language developed especially for learning; adult students may look at CYCLOPS, the Open University's computer-assisted electronic overhead projector. Indeed, next to the use of women's names for computer programs (a practice which also comments on important characteristics of the world of computers), the references to Greek culture are perhaps the most frequent.

The reference to Proteus, then, provides a resonant image of some of the most important ways in which computers are currently perceived. The most significant features appear to be their power, their versatility and their remoteness. These characteristics are also, of course, those of a god, and one is therefore not surprised to find that at least some of the discussion about implications of computers uses theological terminology. Weizenbaum (1982), for instance, wonders whether the computer may be 'inherently anti-human — an invention of the devil'.

Whether it is seen as a god or a devil, the computer is always perceived as powerful, both in its applications in the real world and in its appearances in the more imaginative forms of our culture, particularly in novels and in films. The wilder reaches of science fiction and fantasy lie beyond the scope of this book. The characterization of computers in certain important novels and films may, however, offer revealing clues to their real nature.

Computers and Power

Although there are no computers as we know them in George Orwell's *Nineteen Eighty-Four*, the characteristics of the society there bear a chilling resemblance to the possibilities for totalitarianism that are offered by the enormous power of computers. The fundamental characteristic of the world of *Nineteen Eighty-Four* is that it is an 'information society', in which there is centralized, absolute control over all information, ranging from individual beliefs to knowledge of the past.

In *Nineteen Eighty-Four*, both privacy and history as we know them have ceased to exist. Privacy, and the possibility of thinking for oneself, have been eliminated by advances in what we now call 'information technology':

> with the advent of television, and the technical advance which made it possible to receive and transmit simultaneously on the same instrument, private life came to an end. . . . The possibility of enforcing not only complete obedience to the will of the state, but complete uniformity of opinion on all subjects, now existed for the first time.

Simultaneously with this absolute destruction of privacy, the state in *Nineteen Eighty-Four* maintains total control over the information which reaches its citizens: 'all history was a palimpsest, scraped clean and reinscribed exactly as often as was necessary'. The Ministry of Truth not only alters all factual information to suit its own purposes but also controls absolutely the multiple ways in which people receive information of any kind. It supplies the citizens

> with newspapers, films, textbooks, telescreen programmes, plays, novels — with every conceivable kind of information, instruction or entertainment, from a statue to a slogan, from a lyric poem to a biographical treatise, and from a child's spelling book to a Newspeak dictionary.

Within the parameters of this totalitarian information society', both language and certain social responses bear an uncanny resemblance to developments currently associated with computers. First, the language *Newspeak* has more than a little in common with the language associated with computers and their programs. In its 'harsh sound and a certain wilful ugliness' it resembles some of the more aggressive formulations of computer jargon which were noted in Chapter 1. It is perhaps unfair to note the linguistic similarity between the very name *Newspeak* and the name of a recent computer language called *Smalltalk*. Nevertheless, the absolute functionalism, the removal of all kinds of the ambiguities that mark ordinary and creative discourse, and the insistence on a one-to-one relationship between words and meanings are common both to *Newspeak* and to the kind of language in which computers must be programmed.

Again, the similarity between the violent content of many contemporary games and the delight in violence as a major form of amusement in *Nineteen Eighty-Four* may not be entirely fortuitous. In Orwell's novel, one of Winston's first acts of rebellion against the omnipotent state is to keep a diary, in which his opening entry describes a visit to a film:

> audience much amused by shots of a great huge fat man trying to swim away with a helicopter after him, first you saw him wallowing along in the water like a porpoise, then you saw him through the helicopters gunsights, then he was full of holes and the sea round him turned pink and he sank as suddenly as though the holes had let in the water, the audience shouting with laughter when he sank.

Anyone who has observed the players of the most widespread forms of computer games may recall similar delight as the animated figures are entertainingly destroyed.

In one crucially important respect, however, there is no resemblance between the society of *Nineteen Eighty-Four* and the world made possible by computers. Because Orwell's state does not have computers, it has to use people to carry out most of the complicated control of information; there is thus no problem of the kind of unemployment that is sometimes associated with computerization. But in every other way in which it deals with information, Orwell's state represents one dire, but technically feasible, outcome of the use of computers.

Most of all, the focus in *Nineteen Eighty-Four* on the way in which power is sought for its own sake uncannily resembles the major characteristic of computers. As O'Brien explains it to Winston, 'the Party seeks power entirely for its own sake. We are not interested in the good of others; we are interested solely in power. Not wealth or luxury or long life or happiness: only power, pure power'. It is 'pure power', too that the computer offers, and only the context and the purposes for which it is used will in the long run determine whether or not the increasing computerization of our society will lead towards *Nineteen Eighty-Four*.

Computers and War

As the novel often emphasises, some of the characteristics of *Nineteen Eighty-Four* derive from its being a society whose citizens are led to believe that they are permanently at war with one or another of its enemies. Orwell's representation of such a war has far more in common with certain features of the Second World War than with anything that computers might contribute to military conflict. The links between computers and contemporary forms of warfare — especially the possibility of nuclear war — are, however, one of the most terrifying concerns of a number of recent books and films.

In 1983, John Badham's film *War Games* focused this concern, sometimes crudely but often tellingly. As its title implies, the film explores the connections between the kinds of computer war games played for amusement and those which are played in deadly earnest as part of the process of studying various possible outcomes in the event of nuclear war. The plot hinges on the hypothetical situation that in his search for new computer games, a schoolboy, highly skilled in computers, manages to tap into the American Defence

Department's Wargames computer — without realizing the source of what he thinks is merely another game with even better effects than usual. Nuclear war is avoided at first purely by chance.

Later in the film, the computer program itself, which is called JOSHUA, tries to make the simulations which it constantly plays, occur in real life. Because of the dependence of the American nuclear war machine on interlocked computer systems from which human decisions have been eliminated as far as possible, the final catastrophe can be averted only by making the computer learn that, as with 'Noughts and Crosses', 'the only winning move is not to play'.

The film itself is one among many examples of major fears about the interactions between computers and the possibility of nuclear war. What makes *War Games* perhaps more emblematic than it would otherwise be is the reality in the world outside it. Further conflating reality and fantasy, a new computer game, 'Computer War', based on the film, appeared in 1983; similar games played for amusement include 'Armageddon'.

Other realities include the fact that no computer system is completely secure: 'given time and sufficient motive a determined computer expert can penetrate the security of the most complex system' (Laver, 1980). Recently, in fact, ten young people, using only microcomputers and telephone links, gained entry to American government nuclear laboratory computer banks; one of them was quoted as saying, 'It's really easy to do' (*The Scotsman*, 1983). Nor can computer systems, whether designed for war or other purposes, ever be proved to be entirely free of error. The significance of *War Games*, then, lies not so much in the film itself but rather in the attention that it draws to the enormity of the potential dangers represented by the applications of computers in preparations for nuclear war.

The Frailty of Powerful Computers

Computer failure leading to the possibility of accidental nuclear war is the most horrifying and extreme illustration of the consequences of computer power combined with computer frailty. Short of such a catastrophic outcome, however, other books and films have explored what might happen following the gradual breakdown or sudden failure of an immensely powerful computer system.

One of the most striking of such explorations appears in the representation of HAL, the computer on board the space flight in Stanley Kubrick's *2001: a Space Odyssey*. HAL, the 'latest result in machine intelligence', can mimic or reproduce the activities of the human brain with far greater speed and reliability than the human beings with whom he shares the spaceship. Supposed to be foolproof and incapable of error, he is given the task of controlling the entire operation of the ship. Everything is apparently going well when he appears to make an error, and the crew decide that he must be partially disabled. The extent of the evil that can be caused by the power and frailty of computers is imaged in the malignity with which HAL then proceeds to destroy all but one of the crew.

Obviously the details of the science fantasy of *2001* bear little relation to our own realities. But the representation of HAL remains a potent image of the effect of combining immense power with frailty. One computer expert, commenting on the more serious depiction of computers in science fiction, remarks:

> I am inclined to fear most the HAL scenario. The first AI (artificial intelligence) systems of large capability will have many layers of poorly understood control structure and obscurely encoded 'knowledge'. . . . I would expect the first self-improving AI machines to become 'psychotic' in many ways, and it may take generations of theories and experiments to 'stabilize' them. The problem could become serious if economic incentives to use the unreliable early systems are large — unfortunately there are too many ways in which a dumb system with a huge data base can be useful. (Minsky, 1979).

The social consequences of placing absolute reliance on a computer system which then exhibits increasing degrees of frailty are also depicted powerfully in E. M. Forster's short story, 'The Machine Stops'. As in *Nineteen Eighty-Four*, there are no explicit references to computers, but Forster's vision of an 'information society', like Orwell's nightmare account, bears an often uncanny resemblance to what is becoming increasingly possible with the new information technologies.

In Forster's world, human beings have become entirely dependent on the 'Machine': a term for a kind of integrated system of telecommunications and computers. Early in the story, Forster makes it clear that his characters have become dependent on the Machine to satisfy their physical and psychological needs:

> She generated the light, and the sight of her room, flooded with radiance, revived her. There were buttons and switches everywhere — buttons to call for food, for music, for clothing. There was the hot bath button, by which a basin of (imitation) marble rose out of the floor, filled to the brim with a warm deodorized liquid. There was the cold water button. There was the button that produced literature. And there were of course the buttons by which she communicated with her friends. The room, though it contained nothing, was in touch with all she cared for in the world.

This is not a mere fantasy of the future. Rather, it bears a remarkable resemblance to the description of the 'information society' on the dust jacket of Martin's *The Wired Society*, a factual look at the technical possibilities:

> Imagine yourself absorbed into the world of the future. . . . You lean forward, turn on your 7-foot television screen. You could watch a movie, sports, or news, but instead you decide to see what life is like in another corner of the world. So you turn to the travel agent's channel, select a country, sit back, and watch an array of action views from some exotic land.

> Perhaps you'd like to play chess. Simply punch into the computer in your living room and you have an instant partner.
>
> Want to shop? Turn to the shopper's catalog on the TV dial where you can purchase anything from clothing to computers.
>
> Tomorrow is a work day. After four days of leisure, it's time for three days of work. But there's no need to ... go to the office — just check your computer terminal to see what instructions your boss has left you. If you have any questions you can reach him [sic] by videophone. (Martin, 1978).

Unlike Martin, Forster's concern lies not with the technicalities of such a society, but with the human consequences produced by its extensive dependence on the computer system. The first of these consequences, as he depicts them, is the gradual inability to confront unmediated experience: when she considers actually visiting her son, the chief character is 'seized with the terrors of direct experience'.

Secondly, in Forster's fictional world, the sheer quantity of indirect human interactions has increased dramatically: 'she knew several thousand people; in certain directions human intercourse had advanced enormously'. The quality of so much mediated experience, however, has diminished. 'The Machine did not transmit *nuances* of expression. It only gave a general idea of people — an idea that was good enough for all practical purposes.'

Most serious of all the consequences of using the Machine to mediate all human needs is the insidious way in which people gradually lose control over it, in a way analogous to the fact that there are now some computer programs that no one person entirely understands: 'no one confessed the Machine was out of hand. Year by year it was served with increased efficiency and decreased intelligence. The better a man knew his own duties upon it, the less he understood the duties of his neighbour, and in all the world there was not one who understood the monster as a whole.' Finally, the Machine breaks down, and the society which had become totally dependent on it is also destroyed: man is 'strangled in the garments that he had woven'.

In Forster's story, the computer becomes a kind of god, worshipped for its power, its errors denied. The image, after all, is perhaps not so very far distant from some contemporary visions of the computer as an infallible source of power. Certainly, organizations which use computers extensively have been noticeably reticent about any failures in their systems, including breaches of security: 'a number of cases [of computer fraud] which have been exposed by audit, or revealed by accident, have not been reported to the police or pressed to trial' (Laver, 1980). When this reluctance to admit frailty is combined with the propensity to admire the sheer power of the computer, we may see certain undesirable but plausible images of the computer in the sombre stories of both Forster and Kubrick.

Beyond fiction, there are many fears that have been expressed about the implications of computerizing society. This book does not attempt to consider these in any significant way: in any case, there are already a number of excellent works on the subject, as noted in Appendix 2. But before we can understand the character of contemporary computers we do need at least to note some of the main economic, political and social implications of their increasingly widespread use.

Computers and Economics

The major contemporary anxiety about the economic impact of computers is unquestionably the fear that they will exacerbate unemployment. There are also serious doubts about how far all of the economic benefits of computerization will actually contribute to human welfare. Probable changes in the nature and conditions of work as it will be affected by computers cause both concern and optimism.

Overall, there are no firm conclusions that can be drawn about the long-term effects of computerization on employment. Attitudes towards the short-term effects tend to be highly coloured by political affinities. Trade unions, for instance, generally see the new information technologies, including computers, as a threat. For many members of trade unions, 'new technology is summed up in four R's, redundancy, redeployment, retraining and reduced skills' (Laver, 1980).

On the other hand, for those who believe in the free market economy, the emphasis tends to lie rather on the large numbers of jobs that may be created by the burgeoning industries associated with the new information technologies. More neutral forecasts are not quite so optimistic. The OECD estimates, for instance, that only '60 per cent of the direct reduction of manpower demand imputable to technology will be compensated by 1990' (OECD, 1982). From the world of computer specialists, the following comment emerges: 'we have neither the facts nor the understanding to be able to predict the long-term effects of computers on employment, but short-term increases in unemployment and enforced changes of job seem inevitable' (Laver, 1980).

There is already a considerable body of evidence to suggest that these changes are likely to affect women more adversely than men. It is probable that the most radical changes in employment that will be created by computerization in the near future are those involved in information work of one kind or another, particularly in office work. 'In most industrialized countries ... the reduction of staff predicted in offices and banks is in the region of 30 to 50 per cent' (Trudel and Belanger, 1982). Since the vast majority of workers in these fields are women, it follows that they are most vulnerable to the threat of computer-created unemployment. When such predictions are juxtaposed with the male domination of the computer world already noted in Chapter 1, one may hazard a reasonable guess that without some form of intensive positive action to resolve the problem, women may be economically more disadvantaged by computerization than their male counterparts.

Computerization is already having controversial effects on the value of certain kinds of skills as well as on the conditions in which people work. For instance, those skills of speed, accuracy and neatness on which much traditional female employment has been built are no longer significant: my word processor virtually obliterates the difference between my amateur efforts and those of an excellent professional typist. The net result is to upgrade my own competence and to devalue the skills of the typist.

With computers linked with one another, it is now possible for people to do at home the kind of work that was once confined to offices. The social implications of this economic and often cost-effective possibility are — at best — still controversial. One American study, for instance, has shown that not everyone would necessarily welcome the opportunity of working at home (Laver, 1980). In any case, the prospect is most likely to be available only to those who have adequate space and sufficient domestic support at home.

In all of these examples of the possible economic implications of computerization, however, the effects depend in the final analysis on the purposes for which new technologies are introduced. So far the overwhelming purpose has been to increase productivity and efficiency, thereby cutting costs and labour requirements. Even where these purposes predominate, there are sometimes genuine human benefits from computerization as, for example, when robots undertake dangerous or de-humanizing work previously done by people. In general, the computer technology involved remains neutral, but any serious consideration of its economic implications must take account of the fact that the context within which it is normally introduced tends to stress cost-cutting and profit-making.

Politics and Computers

Over the past few years, a number of concerns have been expressed about some of the political implications of increasing computerization. Two of these issues — those concerning the computer's threat to privacy and the computer's contribution to the possibility of a nuclear war — have already been briefly discussed as they appear in *Nineteen Eighty-Four* and *War Games*, but may require more realistic treatment. There are other concerns, too, about the possible dangers of the trend towards making more and more political decisions based on computer simulations or on other computer-supported information systems.

The very real dangers that the new information technologies pose to a society that values its political democracy have been clearly formulated by Laver (1980):

> The communication and computing services of a society can be regarded as its 'nervous system', whose function it is to tie together its institutions and its people, and to co-ordinate their activities. Better and faster information services inevitably tend to encourage centralization and to promote uniformity, and these in

> turn make it easier to speed up and improve the services given, and so on. This cumulative process could end in total control from the centre.

Already, a considerable volume of information is available about each of us in various government departments and other large and small institutions. Such storage of information frequently takes place, of course, without being placed on computer records. The real danger represented by the computer is the possibility that it offers of collecting more facts together more quickly, and thereby perhaps acquiring a knowledge of our private lives that we would prefer an outsider not to have.

Political decisions depend not only on information of this sort but also increasingly on computer simulations, particularly on those which attempt to model the economy and to provide economic forecasting. The danger here is that 'computer-based mathematical models of the world may come to dominate the judgements of governments and corporations despite their limitations and the uncertainties of their predictions' (Mason, 1983).

The problem is basically that, as Weizenbaum (1979) notes, the computer tends to induce confidence in its results and to magnify effects as was seen in the Vietnam War.

> Admiral Moorer, then Chairman of the Joint Chiefs of Staff, testified to the US Senate Armed Services Committee that specially programmed computers in the field systematically lied to the Pentagon's computers with respect to the secret bombing of Cambodia. It was of course not some computer in the Pentagon that was misled by such lies — computers process information, not meanings — it was the policymaker who relied, or claimed to rely, on 'what the computer says' whose decisions were gravely affected.

But the most sombre of the political implications of computers lie in the connections between computers and preparations for nuclear war. The origins of contemporary computer technologies were predominantly military, and military, particularly nuclear, applications continue to be one of the main purposes to which powerful computers are now dedicated. In most discussions about the political implications of computers, this subject is tactfully avoided. It seems to me, however, that we cannot realistically or morally ignore this central issue of how certain uses of computers threaten our very existence.

There are at least three ways in which computers and associated information technologies have increased the threat of nuclear war. First, the reliance of the nuclear powers on computer-based defence systems has increased the danger that errors in the systems of communication and control could be an important factor in a series of misjudgements or miscalculations that might lead to a nuclear exchange. Second, the greatly enhanced accuracy of computer-based nuclear systems has made it technically feasible to consider using such weapons on the battlefield, at an earlier stage of an escalating conflict than might otherwise have been the case. Finally, as the nuclear powers increasingly rely on computer simulations as the basis for making decisions, there remains at least a metaphorical danger of reducing war to the level of a computer game, in which death becomes merely 'the absence of electronic noise' (Burkitt and Williams, 1980).

Here, as with the economic implications of computers, however, it is not the computers themselves but their contexts and purposes which determine the final effects of using them. The potential power that computers, allied with other new technologies, can give to political leaders is immense, but those leaders — and not the machines themselves — are responsible for how it is used.

Computers in Society

As with the long-term economic or political effects of computerization, it is virtually impossible to predict with any certainty what impact computers will make on our society. Already, however, two broad areas of concern have emerged. First, many commentators have remarked on the probability that, failing attempts to counteract such an effect, computers may increase the fragmentation and even the divisiveness of our society. Secondly, there is a growing body of comment about the seductiveness of computer power.

Full exploitation of the possibilities offered by computers and associated information technologies entails 'a major contradiction: it increases fantastically the technical possibilities of information and knowledge exchange between persons and groups while, at the same time, it reduces the opportunities for direct exchanges, meetings and re-groupings' (Trudel and Belanger, 1982).

Many of the activities of our daily lives that currently involve being with other people are increasingly becoming possible to carry out without having to come into contact with others. Changes in banking have already been noted in Chapter 1, but these are merely the more visible sign of an increasing trend towards providing information and even goods and some services mediated by a computer. The kinds of services that can be provided by cable television, linked with computers, and those which are already available through various telecommunications and computer networks make it increasingly unnecessary to move from home to meet many ordinary needs. The question, however, of whether these technical possibilities will result in increasing isolation is still wide open to debate.

A more pressing and perhaps more disturbing issue is the possibility that computers and associated information technologies will widen still further the gap between our 'Two Nations'. Clearly the issue is one on which one's attitude will depend significantly on one's political affinities. The difficulty is sketched clearly by a computer expert:

> The advance of information technology could . . . make the information-rich even richer, and widen the gulf between them and the information-poor. This is a troublesome possibility because the information-poor will tend to be those

> who are deprived economically and educationally, and who are thus most in need of the benefits that better information could bring. It seems likely that the provision of improved information services will be divisive between human and social groups. (Laver, 1980).

The central fact is that the use of computers and their associated information technologies cost money; the more sophisticated the use, the more significant the amount of money involved. It is not fortuitous that the major banks are computerized while important national voluntary organizations such as the Citizens' Advice Bureaux, which deal with large amounts of information and which could benefit significantly from computerization, are not.

The second major fear often expressed about the social impact of computers stems from the acknowledged seductiveness of using them. There is, for instance, the phenomenon of the (always male) compulsive programmer:

> Wherever computer centres have become established . . . bright young men of disheveled appearance, often with sunken glowing eyes, can be seen sitting at computer consoles, their arms tensed and waiting to fire their fingers, already poised to strike, at the buttons and keys. . . . When not so transfixed, they often sit at tables strewn with computer printouts over which they pore like possessed students of a cabalistic text. They work until they nearly drop, twenty, thirty hours at a time. Their food, if they arrange it, is brought to them: coffee, Coke, sandwiches. If possible, they sleep on cots near the computer. But only for a few hours — then back to the consoles or the printouts. . . . They are oblivious to their bodies and to the world in which they move. They exist . . . only through and for the computers. These are computer bums, compulsive programmers. They are an international phenomenon. (Wiezenbaum, 1976).

It is notable that even someone such as James Martin (1978), who enthusiastically promotes the advantages of the new 'information society', speaks of the 'narcotic spell of programming'. An IBM representative, too, recently referred to a new social problem that is more prevalent than computer backlash: computer addiction (Lean, 1983). Lean goes on to comment that one 'computer widow' has even recorded a song about the problem, 'BASIC Ain't the Language of Love'.

The enhanced sense of personal power that seems to underlie the seductive appeal of computers may also be on of the sources of the pleasure obviously experienced in the computer games which are now prevalent. The social implications of the apparently compulsive nature of many computer games, combined with their frequently violent content, may also cause some unease.

But one needs to make the same important qualification about the social impact of computers that was made about their economic and political implications. There is nothing inherent in the nature of computers that makes it essential to play only violent games on them, nor are computers in themselves responsible for the will to power that often exploits them. These outcomes are determined by people, not machines. But the machines themselves do have certain characteristics that make particular outcomes more likely than others.

The Character of Contemporary Computers

In the broadest terms a computer is simply an electronic machine that can handle very large amounts of information at tremendous speed; it is 'a mindless tool with infinite use' (Radcliffe and Salkeld, 1983). One can perhaps best think of it as a fancy machine that can deal, accurately and untiringly, with almost, any kind of information that can be coded without ambiguity. Thus, computers can respond to any kind of symbol — to words, sounds, images and so on, as well as to numbers. To do so they follow sets of instructions which are known as 'programs', the ubiquitous American spelling being particularly useful to a British audience to distinguish computer programs from other kinds of programmes. These programs are written by people in any one of a variety of languages, depending both on the purpose for which the program is designed and the machine it will be used on.

Computers vary enormously in size — and therefore in the amount of information they can handle — and the speed at which they can do so. They also show an astonishing degree of versatility, so that they can be used, for example, in applications ranging from industrial robots to medical investigations to record keeping to guiding space flights to learning at home. But they all consist basically of only a few main parts: something which puts the information and the programs into them (often called a terminal), a way of processing the information (called the central processing unit), somewhere to store information for later use (often on a disk or a tape) and at least one device to let someone see or otherwise get hold of the information (usually a television-like screen or a printer). Further details about how they operate are so readily available (see Appendix 1) that they do not need to be outlined here.

Computers are often surrounded by a mystique that makes them appear difficult for a novice to use. In fact, depending on how the machine is designed and programmed, many computers can be used for at least some purposes by virtually anyone. In order to use the programs in the public exhibitions, 'Computers for All' in Scotland, for instance, one had merely to insert a disk into the machine and switch it on, an even simpler procedure than playing a record or a vidoe cassette. For more complicated functions, as well, it is often remarkably easy to use computers: my own experience as a novice is that one can learn to use a good word processing program, for instance, in about half an hour, if help is available from a good teacher or a good set of instructions.

The crucial distinction here lies between using the computer and programming it. The former can be made very easy, depending on the design of both the machine and its programs. Actually learning to program at a sophisticated level in one or more serious computer languages is, however, a very different matter, and high levels of specialist training are needed. But it is possible to get a taste of what programming involves by learning a little BASIC on a microcomputer, and this too is a relatively simple process, depending again on the quality of the teaching. So computers basically can be easy to use where people have chosen to make them so, and for most practical purposes most of us will not actually need to program them ourselves.

But the character of contemporary computers has also to be seen in the context of the new information technologies that are often associated with them. Indeed, as Laver (1980) notes, 'communicating and computing are . . . complementary functions in automatic information systems, and there is no longer much point in drawing a distinction between them'. What is most significant is that between them, computers and telecommunications represent an explosive increase in our ability to handle information.

For general purposes, the precise methods by which these interlocked technologies work are relatively unimportant (except to computer engineers). The non-expert who is interested in the ways that computers can be used and the implications of doing so simply does not require a detailed account of the inner workings of computers. The question of exactly how much one has to know about computers before being able to make a sound judgement about their applications and implications is much debated, however. I shall consider it further in Chapter 4, as part of the discussion about the nature of computer literacy.

For the time being, it can be recognised that contemporary computers do make possible the kinds of consequences discussed throughout this chapter. Whether they come to fruition, or whether we insist that computers should first of all meet human needs is our decision. Much of the alienation from computers that is often experienced by adults today is wholly unnecessary. It arises partly because those who design and implement computer systems do not take sufficient account of the needs of the people with whom those system will interact, partly because it is usually cheaper in the short run to ignore such needs. But there are also those institutions which may prefer the mystification often produced by computers as a screen behind which they can protect themselves from public accountability.

In themselves, computers can be many things to many people. They may indeed, be a kind of Golem, who was initially depicted as a perfect and powerful servant whose only fault lay in being too literal, or in too mechanical a fulfillment of his orders. As the Jewish legends associated with Golem developed, however, this clay image brought to life by a charm (much perhaps as the computer, now built basically on the sand of silicon, is brought to life by its program) became increasingly frightening where insufficient human control was exerted over him. It may in the end be this image, rather than that of Proteus, which most computers resemble.

Regardless of one's final assessment of the character of the computer, the power that it provides through the fast, accurate and untiring handling of information and the relative ease with which it can be used mean that there are likely to be some important problems in adult education with which it might be able to help. In itself, of course, the very existence of such a powerful tool implies that adult educators will need to take account of, and respond to, the enormous need for computer literacy for adults; this issue is considered at some length in Chapter 4. Meanwhile, Chapter 3 will look at some ways in which computers may be able to help adult educators more easily to meet certain needs in adult learning.

3

Learning with Computers

I perceive the computer to be the most potent tool for adult learning to appear in modern history

(Malcolm Knowles, 1983)

The potency and the potential of the computer in adult learning are created by many interacting factors. As we have already seen, the computer in itself is an extraordinarily powerful and versatile tool which anyone who cares about learning would be rash to dismiss lightly. The astonishing growth of interest in, and even purchase of, computers over the past few years in Britain, suggests that many people, becoming aware of the power of computers, want to understand the nature and implications of that power and, if possible, to use it for their own ends. Computers, in other words, have become increasingly attractive and desirable (often in sexual terms, if one is to judge by advertisements!). However suspect this desirability may be on moral or social grounds, computers do represent an impressive force, and may therefore be an effective medium to reach out to substantial numbers of women and men.

Moreover, there appears to be a good fit between certain characteristics of computers and some of the ways in which adults learn: although it is limited and highly specific, this fundamental compatibility has already encouraged some adult educators to start exploring territory that is becoming increasingly familiar in schools and in industry. Many of these pioneering ventures have been stimulated by the excitement of what computers can do rather than, perhaps, by what adult educators might want or need them to do. Despite this emphasis, enough new territory has now been cleared for us to see that — for adult learners — the computer is not merely a solution looking for problems to solve.

Problems Amenable to Help by Computers

Above all, computers are a potent tool for adult learning because they offer possible solutions to several major problems within adult education. There are naturally many chronic difficulties which they do not address and which, indeed, they may even exacerbate, depending on the context and purposes of their use. The fact that computers remain relatively expensive, for instance,

SCEMP

Scottish Community Education Microelectronics Project

EDUCATIONAL PROGRAMS

Educational Games — **by the Scottish Microelectronics Development Programme**

There are five options: Spelling Game; Reaction Timer; Counting Game; Fishy Facts; and Solar Distance. You choose one, and enjoy games with an educational basis, and plenty of pictures to help you along.

Sports Quiz — **by Bishopbriggs High School**

There are ten options: Badminton; Basketball; Bowls; Cricket; Soccer; Rugby League; Rugby Union; Golf; Hockey; Ice Hockey. You choose one sport and answer ten true/false questions. Your percentage score is given at the end.

The Shapes Game — **by R A Sparkes of St Andrews College, Glasgow**

This program uses a Concept Keyboard, a flat keypad which plugs into the Apple. This program secretly chooses one of the shapes on the concept keyboard, and then invites you to guess which shape it is. You press one of the shapes, and the program guides you by hints on the screen, until you manage to get the right shape, colour and size, either by random guessing or by logical reasoning.

Spellstring — **by the Scottish Microelectronics Development Programme**

This is a program which lets you look again at those areas in spelling that give trouble to old and young alike, for example, "le" and "kn".

Road Safety Quiz — **by Stuart Roebuck**

This program allows you to choose questions on a topic or on a combination of topics (from a list of 17, e.g. Pedestrians, Motorcycles, Parking). Your percentage score is given at the end of each set of 10 true or false questions. (The program allows adaptation to other subject areas.)

What Day Is It? — **by SCEMP**

Using a well-known rhyme, this program makes learning how to use a calendar fun.

A taste of individualized learning for adults.

does nothing to alleviate the serious under-funding of nearly all adult education in Britain; indeed, as we have just seen in Chapter 2, the costs involved in computing may lead to even greater divisiveness wherever the market economy prevails. But computers as an educational tool also have the power to help ease certain important problems for adult learners.

In the first place, adult education as traditionally made available in Britain has often been unable to provide adequately for the very diverse needs of its participants. There are many people who actively prefer anonymity to personal contact; there are others who learn best within a highly structured environment rather than the more informal arrangements that prevail in many learning groups. These often dramatic differences in learning styles are generally awkward, if not impossible, to accommodate within many traditional modes of adult education. In this context, the flexibility and versatility of the computer can enlarge the options from which adults with different learning styles may choose.

For many others, particularly those who have heavy personal or professional responsibilities or those who live outside major cities, practical difficulties of time and space are often a barrier to taking part in learning activities designed to suit a majority of other students. The importance of providing distance learning for such students is, of course, now widely recognized, and there is a substantial and growing amount of material available for them. Computer programs are potentially one of the most valuable additions to such materials for distance learning: it is no coincidence that a number of the institutions most committed to distance learning — the Open University, the BBC and the National Extension College — make increasing use of them.

Computers, then, can help to dismantle practical barriers of time and space which could otherwise debar adults from certain kinds of learning. And as we have seen, they offer a potentially attractive variety of ways to help resolve the educational quandary of diverse learning styles. Combined with their other educational implications, these possible advantages would in themselves justify adult educators in taking them seriously.

But there are other problems, too, for which adult education has not yet found any satisfactory resolution. There are substantial numbers of people — particularly young men in the lower socio-economic groups — who appear to take little, if any, part in adult education (see ACACE, 1982a). As yet there has been no substantial study of the socio-economic composition of people who are attracted to using computers where they are freely accessible, but there is a growing body of evidence that young men in the lower socio-economic groups may be very attracted to using computers as a medium for virtually anything, including learning.

Both the BBC's Computer Literacy Project and the 'Prestel for People' project have recently found that men in lower socio-economic groups are more attracted to using computers than one might have predicted from their very low rate of participation in adult education (see Radcliffe and Salkeld, 1983; Kania, 1983). My own experience at public exhibitions of computers is that young men in particular seemed very eager to use the machines even for programs that appeared to be well beyond their educational level. Unpublished work with young offenders also seems to suggest that they particularly like using computers as an educational medium (Home Office, 1983).

In the areas of adult basic education and of health education, public bodies have already expressed their faith in the possibilities of using computers to reach many people who have shunned more traditional modes of adult education. Thus a number of bodies involved in health education in Scotland have sponsored or provided computer programs about solvent abuse, using alcohol, healthy eating and stopping smoking (SCEMP, 1983). In adult basic education, too, the sheer attractiveness of computers has led a number of workers to explore how they can take advantage of the fact that many students seem to prefer such a medium (see, for instance, SCEMP, 1983, and ALBSU, 1982).

Finally, the path of adult learning is often littered with good intentions or brave attempts that do not reach the intended destination: many adults embark on learning projects which they do not complete. I am not suggesting that computers can solve this complex problem. There are often reasons for dropping out that are so powerful (such as increased pressure at work or at home) that the only way to stay sane is to yield to them, at least for a time. In other cases, adults discover that the particular education they have undertaken is uncongenial or leads them in directions they prefer not to go. But there are some cases in which — particularly where other factors in their lives may not be conducive to prolonged study — adults are discouraged from learning because they have to wait so long for feedback from tutors. As the National Extension College has already shown, providing computerized marking for students' work seems virtually to eliminate drop-out rates on correspondence courses (Freeman, 1983).

Experience in the Scottish Community Education Microelectronics Project seems to suggest more generally that using computers increases the motivation to persist in learning. In one community education centre providing adult basic education by way of a computer, 'youths, who were haphazard in their attendance, came regularly . . . ; the computer motivated the students to learn and increased their attention span' (SCEMP, 1983).

The simple fact is that for all kinds of adults computers are a popular way of learning. We have already seen in Chapter 1 how very enthusiastic the general public response has been to using computers for learning. Virtually all of the evidence from specific groups of learners also suggests that they delight in using computers. In a project at Alberta College in Canada, for instance, 92 per cent of the hearing-impaired students who used a computerized learning system rated themselves as 'very enthusiastic' about their experience (Loyer, 1983), while in Aylesbury Prison in England, young offenders expressed a marked preference for using a computer over other methods of mastering literacy and numeracy (Home Office, 1983).

There are also a number of other areas in support of adult education in which computers can help to solve endemic problems. As we shall see in Chapter 5, using computers can provide significant help in trying to match adults' educational needs and situations with available resources; computers can also give expert advice in areas in which no specialist personal help is available in any one institution; they can provide enhanced communication which opens new doors to educational experiences for disabled students, and so on.

There are, then, a number of problems, both within and in support of adult learning with which computers can offer limited and specific but effective help. The present chapter will consider three of these kinds of help in some detail: individualized instruction — in which individual students progress through prepared material at a level and a pace that best suits them; learning by discovery — in which students use simulations and models to discover new ideas and concepts or to explore the consequences of their own ideas; and unhampered learning — in which students carry out many tasks liberated from the unnecessary work they would have had to perform had they not used a computer.

Before we consider these possibilities in detail, however, we need to glance at public expectations of learning with computers. Is there any evidence that people in general expect computers to be used for learning? As with virtually every other question in this field, there are as yet no real answers. But the evidence so far does seem to suggest that there is a popular belief that computers have potential educational value. Cynics may argue that the belief is merely the creation of computer firms who believe they can sell more computers by encouraging people to believe that they have educational value.

Regardless of how the belief arises, however, there is evidence that it is there. Two-thirds of all the users of the highly popular BBC Computer, for instance, 'bought them with some educational purpose in mind' (Radcliffe and Salkeld, 1983). In my personal experience, most people who buy a computer for use at home include education as amongst their justifications — even if their idea of education only amounts to self defence against their children's ever-increasing computer literacy!

This popular expectation that computers are educational would in itself justify adult educators experimenting with such a powerful and versatile tool. Many of the current popular expectations of the educational value of computers are inflated and unrealistic. But the very belief in their use as an educational tool does open a tantalizing opportunity for adult education to start to provide the programs that will make the belief more nearly congruent with reality.

Current Developments in Computer Programs for Adults

Because of the constraints on developments that are discussed throughout this book, computer programs for adults are as yet relatively undeveloped, although a few organizations and institutions have taken important steps towards using them for adult learning. Probably the most extensive development of computer programs designed specifically for adults has taken place at the Open University, which has pioneered a variety of important methods for using computers with adult students in specific courses. The BBC is also producing a steadily expanding list of programs for adults, although most of them are educative and useful rather than directly educational. On a much smaller scale, the Scottish Community Education Microelectronics Project has developed programs to demonstrate some of the possibilities of using computers for adult learning.

There have also been many programs created by educators for their own local purposes (see, for instance, Bostock and Seifert, 1983a), and a number of organizations, such as the National Extension College, are currently in the process of developing educational programs. There are several commercial sources of programs specifically designed for adults, such as the PLATO system, which are widely used in North America and are starting to appear more widely in Britain.

As we shall see later in this chapter, there is very little formal evaluation of these programs and much of the comment on them will necessarily be speculative. It is worth noting, indeed, that many of them would not be susceptible to conventional evaluation in any case, as they often have to meet a variety of aims, not all of which are educational. The characteristics of the programs created by and for the Scottish Community Education Microelectronics Project, for instance, result from a variety of purposes including the expediency of finding someone who would create them in the first place, the need to use them for demonstration purposes in public exhibitions and the desire to familiarize people with computers in general (McDonald, 1983c). In other words, they are not fully educational material: they have not been created in response to manifest educational needs; they are not set in any specific educational context: and they have not yet been subject to an assessment of their educational value.

Despite the constraints on development, programs to date show how extraordinarily varied the subjects of computer programs for adults can be. The range of programs available in SCEMP in 1983, for example, included health education, management of personal finances, logical reasoning, quizzes on sports and road safety, local information, introductions to using computers for word processing and for controlling household equipment, and adult basic education (SCEMP, 1983). Within the Open University all faculties have made use of computers in their courses, although as one might expect, science, technology and mathematics have used them more extensively than arts, social science and education. The BBC's computer material for adults included, in 1983, programs to introduce some of the many facilities of the computer, home finance and programs to help with writing programs (Radcliffe and Salkeld, 1983). For local adult education classes, computer programs have been created to teach economics, industrial relations and biological sciences (Bostock and Seifert, 1983a). The National Extension College already has a computer program for use in marking its correspondence courses, and is planning future developments in typing (Freeman, 1983) and other areas.

Already, then, there is a wide range of subjects for which computer programs are being used in adult learning. The actual educational experience offered by these programs is also highly varied, although it seems to fall into three main types: individualized instruction, simulation and unhampered learning. What is each of these, and what do they have to offer to adult learners? And which seem to be particularly promising avenues for further development? It is to these questions that I shall now turn, before moving on to consider the difficult matter of assessing quality in this burgeoning field.

Computers and Individualized Instruction

Computer programs which offer individualized instruction have immediate and obvious possibilities in certain kinds of training, as will briefly be considered later, but they also offer possible advantages to adult learners in introducing them to new material, reinforcing learning by providing a chance to practise and to revise and diagnosing weaknesses. Because of their origins in 'programmed learning' with its behavourist associations, many educators understandably feel uneasy about using them without perhaps fully appreciating exactly what they can offer. A further source of unease arises from the 'cost-effective' arguments that have sometimes been used to justify the use of such programs, the implication being that they can provide teaching more cheaply than it can be done by people. As I hope to show below, neither of these sources of unease is really justified if the programs are used sensitively as an enhancement of learning rather than as the sole means available.

To give the flavour of how individualized instruction or tutorials work, I shall look first at an example of a program used at university level — an Open University program called CICERO — and then at a program, designed for use by the general public, on diminishing one's risk of a heart attack — part of a SCEMP program called 'Health Matters'. Both of these programs allow the people who use them to choose their answers at important points and thereby to influence the next stages or the final outcome of the program; in other words, they teach different people differently, albeit within fairly strict limits.

CICERO, which was designed to provide students with feedback, diagnostic assessment and remedial help, was evaluated during its use on the Open University course, *Biological Bases of Behaviour*, by Scanlon *et al.* (1982), from whom the following summary is taken. For each computer tutorial, questions relating to a specific part of the course were sent in advance to students to answer at home; these questions which were usually multiple-choice, diagnosed the student's conceptual strength and weakness in specific objectives of that part of the course. The student then took the completed answers to his or her study centre, and used the computer terminal there to type the answers in. The program could then ask additional questions to verify the diagnosis. Then, according to the student's answers, the program provided advice and remedial help. A similar system, called 'Merlin', but complete with the help of a human tutor over a telephone link, was used by students in the course *Images and Information*.

Students' response to these programs suggest that they appreciated this computerized learning because it provided a new approach to the subject, individual teaching, a precis of the unit, more course material, a tutor who couldn't get sidetracked, immediate feedback and a means to make learning fun. They also remarked on the advantages of the self-assessment generated by the system as well as the fact that it found and corrected weak points and generally provided extra help. The perceived disadvantages nearly all related to difficulties in getting to the program in the first place, such as over-booking of terminals, inconvenient times, uncertainty about instructions for use and so on.

SCEMP's community education program, 'Health Matters', also tries to diagnose and remedy potential weaknesses, in this case health hazards. Part of this program enables anyone using it to assess his or her risk from a heart attack. The program begins with an introduction on how to use the computer for those who want detailed advice about use. It then allows the learner to calculate his or her risk from a heart attack by entering details of such factors as heredity, exercise, age, weight, use of tobacco and amount of animal fats eaten. Finally, there is advice tailored to each specific learner about how his or her risk of heart attack could be diminished, and there is a chance to go on to explore some ways of improving one's chances by altering one's diet. Throughout, the learners can choose which parts of the program they want to do, and can see the implications of their life styles. As with the Open University programs, adult learners seem to have responded favourably, although SCEMP has not yet carried out a full evaluation of its programs.

Meanwhile, the area of health education appears to offer considerable scope for further development of this kind of program, and SCEMP has explored a number of possibilities, in conjunction with various organizations committed to health education. So far SCEMP has produced or adapted five programs in health education for adults, as may be seen in the illustrations opposite. Each of them is attractive and easy to use, providing learners with the chance to explore the implications of the health choices they have made. As SCEMP has discovered, it is often difficult in creating such programs to satisfy the very different criteria applied to them by health educators, computer programmers and the general public (SCEMP, 1983). Nevertheless, the general response seems to be highly favourable: on the one occasion on which a Health Board required all users to record their responses, all learners reported that they found the health programs either very or fairly interesting,

SCEMP

Scottish Community Education Microelectronics Project

HEALTH PROGRAMS

Infant Feeding — **by Edinburgh University**

This program has been written with expectant mothers in particular in mind but should be of interest to all women at whatever stage in family life. It lets you explore the whole controversy about the "best" method of feeding a new baby and in doing so, explodes some of those old wives' tales.

Stopping Smoking? — **by the Scottish Health Education Group, in collaboration with SCEMP**

There are four options. What Will I Gain If I Stop Smoking; How Can I Stop Smoking; Can Smoking Damage my Health; and Questions on Stopping Smoking. The advantages of giving up smoking are spelled out clearly, and useful hints are offered on how to go about it.

Health Awareness Games — **by Dr Lynda Ellis and Dr Michael Hendry**

There are five options: Coronary Risk; Smoking; Exercise Weight; Life Expectancy; and Lifestyle. The user is asked to give personal details, and then the program uses these details to feed back health information and advice, in written and in graphic form.

Alochol and Health — **by Argyll and Clyde Health Board in collaboration with SCEMP**

The program shows how it is possible to drink socially without ill-effects. There is particular emphasis on the amount that you can sensibly drink without your health being harmed.

Health Matters — **by SCEMP**

This program helps you to assess your risk of a heart attack, and looks at the effect of diet on your health.

SCEMP Health programs.

and over 70 per cent believed that they had learned something of value from them (SCEMP, 1982a).

The other area which looks particularly promising for extensive developments in individualized computer learning for adults is that of adult basic education. We have already seen how attractive learning by computer appears to be to many adults who are trying to learn basic skills, and throughout all parts of Britain workers in adult basic education have been experimenting with the use of computer programs to teach a variety of skills, mainly numeracy and literacy, but also such very specific skills as form filling and reading calendars.

Because of the widespread interest in this field, the Adult Literacy and Basic Skills Unit set up an advisory group to examine the use of microcomputers in basic education. Initially, the group was more impressed by what it perceived as the serious disadvantages rather than the more trivial advantages of using computers in adult basic education; however,

> many of the Group's original fears and reservations about the use of microcomputers in basic education were allayed after seeing the students using microcomputers. Having seen the use to which microcomputers were applied, their motivating power and the flexibility that accompanied well-prepared programs, there emerged a feeling within the group that microcomputers, although still only an aid to learning, were qualitatively different from other 'aids', (ALBSU, 1982).

ALBSU also uncovered an unexpected strength of interest in the use of microcomputers for adult basic education: of the 90 questionnaires that it sent out, 105 were returned, and the two national workshops which were mounted in 1982 were heavily oversubscribed. Amongst workers in adult basic education, there would appear to an enormous amount of interest in the possibilities of using computers with their students. But what, aside from their obvious appeal to basic learners, might computer programs in this area have to offer?

In theory, at least, this kind of individualized learning could be particularly effective in developing basic skills such as literacy and numeracy, where careful presentation of new material at a rate suited to each individual could greatly assist in building up the skills and confidence necessary to undertake the next stages. The opportunities provided by computers simply to practise newly acquired skills and to get immediate feedback about them are also obviously of potential value.

But it is by no means yet certain that such programs can yield better results in educational performance than more conventional methods. There are a number of enthusiastic American reports about the dramatic increases in educational performance wrought by using computers in teaching numeracy and literacy, but many British educators remain sceptical (see Hawkridge, 1983b). A recent evaluation of an anglicized version of the literacy and numeracy parts of PLATO's Adult Basic Learning Skills System carried out in Aylesbury

Prison for the Home Office concluded that there was no significant overall difference in the educational performance of learners taught by the computerized system, but there was a significant difference in the attitudes of the young offenders, who overwhelmingly preferred to learn with the computer (Home Office, 1983).

ALBSU also remains very aware of the constraints as well as the possible virtues of using computers in basic education for adults. The final report emphasizes that

> although microcomputers can have an effective role to play in basic education, their effectiveness relies heavily upon sufficient knowledge and skill in structuring their use and in evaluating the strengths and weakness of programs. . . . When used as an element in a balanced learning programme, microcomputers presented an exciting range of possibilities for many students. (ALBSU, 1982).

In other areas of adult learning as well, there is obviously wide scope for developing more programs of a similar kind, as may be seen from the titles of SCEMP's other programs, and from the many programs available in schools for various forms of individualized instruction in most subjects in the curriculum. Despite the often serious reservations which many educators feel about any overly extensive use of them, the favourable response that they nearly always encounter from the learners themselves suggests that they may be one valuable way of enhancing adult learning.

It must be stressed, however, that there is no evidence that computers can or should replace, as opposed to supplementing, the availability of other people both as fellow learners and as tutors. All the evidence points to the fact that computerized individual instruction is — at best — no more than equally effective as an alternative to traditional instruction (see, for instance, Home Office, 1983; Hooper, 1977; Hawkridge, 1983a).

Moreover, for many forms of adult learning it is simply not appropriate to offer such highly individualized tuition on its own: groups of adults who are learning together to understand their political and social lives or who are sharing their experiences of reading nineteenth-century novels are unlikely to want individualized computer programs! Overall, for adult learners the main advantages of individualized learning with computers may very well be simply that for certain specific subjects and skills, the computer is remarkably popular as an educational medium.

In certain forms of industrial and practical training, however, there is growing use of such methods as a substitute for the presence of other students and tutors. Individualized instruction can have obvious advantages for large, geographically spread-out organizations who continually wish to train and up-date various skills at local level without the expense and difficulty of arranging travel, accommodation and so on. It is thus not surprising that such systems of computerized instruction are already widely used in large organizations, initially in North America and increasingly in Britain.

The kinds of training that may be offered by individualized computer

Computers and training: PLATO in use.

instruction naturally include instruction in how to use computers themselves. Let me cite a homely example. Like most home computers, the one on which I am currently working came with an introductory program which uses the computer to teach how to use the computer (even though many of the things that it teaches me how to do are not entirely useful for writing books!).

This use of the computer to teach how to use the computer is probably one of the most widespread methods of computer training. Some of the most popular courses currently on offer in the PLATO system of individualized instruction in Britain are courses in how to use computer keyboards, courses in how to sell computers and a course about the impact of computers in the workplace. But the ideas are clearly adaptable to almost any kind of training that can be effectively broken down into small segments amenable to sequential treatment or that requires mastery of considerable amounts of information that may be related to one another in complex ways.

There are therefore possibilities for adults learning by individualized computer instruction for both education and training (which are, of course, not exclusive but rather mutually enriching). So far, these kinds of possibilities are perhaps the ones that most adult educators may have encountered in schools, colleges, community organizations, and training establishments. But more educationally exciting possibilities arise through the development of ways in which computers can help adult learners to discover new ideas and information through the use of simulations and models.

Computers and Learning by Discovery

There are already a number of highly sophisticated computer programs which simulate situations or areas of knowledge about which it would be difficult or even dangerous to acquire familiarity or understanding in other ways. In the social and natural sciences in particular there are obvious advantages in having computer programs which can allow students to experiment and to discover the consequences of their theories without actually having to carry out often tedious and time-consuming experimental work. In the study of genetics, a computer program can now be used which simulates genetic effects in successive generations, without the need to wait for such natural events to occur in the laboratory. In nuclear engineering one can carry out experiments on the behaviour of nuclear reactors under various conditions, at least some of which would not be safe to test in practice. In the training of medical students there are sound ethical and professional reasons for allowing students to choose different courses of action and have the consequences of their choices simulated on computer programs rather than on live patients.

Similarly, adult students can evaluate their own understanding and assessment of the variables in the macro-economy by using a computer model, such as that described by Bostock and Seifert (1983a):

> In one particular game of the national economy the students were put in the

> positions of Chancellor of the Exchequer and told that they could alter some (but not all) variables at the start of each year. The students were divided into small groups, each with direct access to the microcomputer. Each group was provided with initial values for the main economic variables (e.g. rate of interest, money supply, tax burden). The game they were then asked to play was a deterministic simulation with discrete time intervals of five years. The students were asked to predict the movement in output, inflation and employment given changes in other variables based on their knowledge of key economic concepts such as the multiplier. The students typed into the computer their assessment of what is required to achieve stated economic objectives, for example a balanced budget, and the program calculates and shows the effect of these policies. The program stores the current state of the economy as each group sees it so that the groups use the program simultaneously but independently. The process is repeated until a General Election is called when each group can assess its performance within the class.

The advantages that Bostock and Seifert claim for this use of a model of the economy is that it helps students to grasp the dynamic interactions of certain key economic concepts and gives them some insight into decision-making procedures within major institutions such as the Treasury. Since complex computer models are in fact used in the making of major national decisions on defence, the economy and so on, clearly their use in adult education may help students better to understand the society around them.

The kinds of simulations currently available in America include a strikingly large and varied range, including ones that illustrate the dilemma of solid-waste disposal, family dynamics, the rabbit population, urban growth, heroin addiction and its impact on the community (Roberts and Anderson, 1983). Within Britain computer simulations and models include flight simulators for training of pilots, in which the pilot can be presented with more unusual emergencies than he or she would presumably hope ever to encounter in real life (Ross, 1980). There are many other kinds of computer models, such as ones for price elasticity and manpower planning (Bostock and Seifert, 1983a). Within training, large numbers of computer simulations are used in military establishments (Hooper, 1977), and there have been a number of developments in using simulations to train technicians in fault-finding in electronic circuits (see Hooper, 1977; and Howe, n.d.).

As with the use of computers for individualized instruction, there are, of course, significant reservations about exactly how valuable computer simulations and models may be for adult learning. Where complex social phenomena are involved, computer models will obviously represent only approximations to reality. As Shubik (1979) remarks, 'it is easy to build a large-scale simulation of virtually anything; but it is difficult to determine if the simulation provides a good model of any particular firm, city, country or other organism.'

With some models, too, the assumptions on which they are constructed may not always be apparent to the learners, who may thus unknowingly absorb unsustainable or unjustifiable models of reality. When they are used for training, computer simulations may not provide sufficient practical experience and may induce a feeling of false confidence. Where they are carefully created so that their premises are examinable and where they are used with discretion and care, however, computer models and simulations may be both exciting and valuable ways of enhancing adult learning.

Computers and Unhampered learning

Both individualized instruction and simulations of models are therefore good examples of where, if used carefully, computers can enhance adult learning. The third area, however, is somewhat less easily categorized, although it may ultimately have an even more significant impact on adult learning.

This third area is perhaps most simply defined as that in which computers reduce the unnecessary workload of students. Anyone who has ever undertaken serious study will be conscious of a distinction (drawn by McDonald *et al.*, 1977) between authentic labour — those things one has to do as an integral part of learning and which make a valuable contribution to it — and inauthentic labour — the work that is undertaken because it makes learning possible but which is not integral for learning and which is not valued for its own sake.

An obvious example of this distinction might be the tedious process of finally getting hold of an elusive but important book as differentiated from the stimulating process of actually coming to grips with the ideas in it. Analogously, physically copying out the final version of an essay merely to enable a tutor to read what would otherwise have been a messy scrawl can be contrasted with the genuine work of wrestling with the ideas that created the essay in the first place.

Computers are already capable of greatly reducing this inauthentic labour that often accompanies learning; they can thus free learners from unnecessary constraints. Using a computer for word processing, for instance, can dramatically shorten the distance between the conception and birth of academic writing. Readers may wonder if what they are reading is any sound demonstration of the benefits, but this book could not have been written at all within the time available had I not used a computer to create the first draft, modify it and finally print out a copy fit to send to the publisher.

For non-experts like myself, using computers for word processing is not entirely straightforward: there are still some things that I think my computer should be able to do with my text that I simply cannot work out how to do. And the fluency that word processing is often reputed to bring to writing can too often become verbosity, because of the sheer ease of actually writing so many words (as readers will no doubt have noticed!). But the time and struggle needed to create a book have been noticeably reduced, in the same way as they would be for any student writing essays or any tutor preparing course material.

Much the same comments apply to using computers to carry out other kinds of manipulation of information. Thus students can make use of the computer as a sophisticated calculator which will take away the tedium of arithmetic and allow them to consider a much wider range of figures than they could otherwise cope with. They can use library computer services to track obscure references rather than tediously making enquiries from many different sources. They can search quickly for the accurate information about travel that is available on the computerized television information services such as Ceefax, Oracle, and Prestel, rather than waiting until the telephone lines are free and an airline or a railway or a bus company finally answers its telephone.

While the two other areas of learning with computers raise serious questions about their educational implications, this use of computers to reduce inauthentic learning seems almost entirely advantageous for adults (unless, of course, one is romantically attached to the idea that the paths to learning ought all to be as difficult as possible!) The use of a computer as a slave which can ease unnecessary human labour seems one important way in which we can all be freed for the genuine pursuit of learning.

An analgous way in which computers can contribute to adult learning is by making it possible for people to learn how to learn. Both in America and Britain children are already using a computer language called LOGO to help them to see cause and effect, to perceive relationships, and to work out for themselves the most effective ways of solving certain kinds of problems (see, for instance, Papert, 1980: Ross, 1980; Hawkridge, 1983a, among many others). In using LOGO, children embark on an exploration of how they think, so that their learning becomes more active and self-directed; they acquire knowledge for a recognized personal purpose (Papert, 1980). So far there has been little use of such possibilities for enhancing adults' learning and reasoning skills by computer programs, but as we shall see further in Chapter 6, this is clearly territory which is ripe for exploration and development.

Meanwhile, it may be that at least some of the mental processes involved in programming computers even at an elementary level could encourage certain modes of thinking that could enrich the possibilities of creative thought. Computers are ruthlessly logical machines that will do, for all practical purposes, only what they are told to do. The very processes of creating even an elementary computer program or of discussing with a programmer what one wants a computer to do require careful, logical thinking that breaks a problem down into its constituent parts and clearly specifies the end to be achieved. Obviously, this computer-like thinking is dehumanizing and restrictive when applied universally, but the practice of engaging in it sometimes may very well sharpen the analytical tools by which other learning problems can be dealt with.

Learning with computers, then, offers a number of ways of enhancing adult learning by building on the enormous strengths of the machines and their programs. Computers can provide individualized learning tailored to different people's different preferences; they can make it possible to study phenomena otherwise difficult to experiment on; and they can strengthen learners in learning how to learn, as well as removing the tedium of much inauthentic learning. But if these promises are to be more fully realized than they now are, adult educators will have to play a more dominant role in the creation of computer programs that genuinely enhance adult learning. The following section will consider how they might start to do so.

Creating Computer Programs for Adults

Despite the exciting possibilities of these kinds of learning with computers, virtually every commentator on computer education remarks on the dearth of good programs for children; good computer programs for adults are even scarcer. As yet, there are few adult educators who are also highly skilled computer programmers, and even fewer computer programmers who seem to have much understanding of how adults learn (see Knowles, 1983). Moreover, opportunities for transforming computer programmers into adult educators or vice versa are very rare and likely to remain so for at least the next few years, until the trainers themselves in both fields become more familiar with the needs and how they might be met. How, in the meantime, are good computer programs for adults likely to be created?

The major way ahead here seems to be for adult educators to take the initiative in approaching programmers with ideas for possible programs, to work closely with them during the development, and then to be able to assess how far the completed results are likely to be acceptable to adults. Because adults, as we have seen, do not immediately take to computers as a learning medium with the same facility as children, programs specifically designed for adults perhaps need to have even higher standards than those created for children. Only adult educators are likely to ensure that such standards are achieved; certainly, as Knowles (1983) suggests, the present learning standards of computer manuals and guides do not inspire any confidence that the computer industry will provide such standards of its own accord.

The experience of the Scottish Community Education Microelectronics Project may perhaps be helpful here. Using both adult educators and computer experts, SCEMP recognized at an early stage that 'programming for the general public, either for use in community settings or for distance learning, requires an additional veneer which is not yet a normal practice amongst programmers' (SCEMP, 1982c). Because they are less familiar with the computer as a medium, for instance, adults are less resilient than children about coping when things appear to go (or actually do go) wrong with a computer program, and they are less tolerant of poor instructions about how to use them. Their unfamiliarity with computers also tends to make them less adventurous in their use, so that they may use whatever program is immediately available on the machine rather than asking for an alternative; where they do select programs from a list, they will tend to choose subjects that are familiar, with titles that sound easy or amusing (ibid).

As a result of the experience of its initial 'Computers for All' exhibitions, SCEMP created 'Guidelines for the Design of Computer Programs for Community Use', a pamphlet which would make useful reading for any adult educator who is interested in working together with programmers to create material for adults. This pamphlet concludes with a 'Checklist for Programs' which provides an illuminating set of questions to ask about any computer programs one is considering for possible use with adults.

The mere fact that some of the questions in these 'Guidelines' need to be asked at all reflects the currently underdeveloped state of creating programs for adults: the questions include asking whether the text is legible, the graphics clear, and whether the spelling, grammar and punctuation are correct! To those who are unfamiliar with the sheer work involved in creating computer programs, such questions will no doubt seem almost grotesquely naive or at least so elementary as to be self evident.

In fact, there are many programs currently in public use which do not fulfil even such basic requirements. This problem is not the result of indifference on the part of the programmer. Rather, it appears to arise because the solution of the programming difficulties is often so all-absorbing that programmers who are not also educators tend to lose interest in those parts of the presentation of their ideas that do not represent programming challenges. Too many programs thus fail to make the instructions to the learners completely clear; or they simply provide mysterious messages at certain points because the computer is not programmed to take account of certain unusual responses. Programs also often fail to require consistent responses from the learner: there are many which ask one to reply sometimes with the entire word 'yes', sometimes simply with the code 'Y', sometimes with a single number chosen from a series of options; and they fail to specify which kind of choice is to be made at which point.

To many programmers such details are trivial and insignificant beside the delights of solving difficult challenges in programming. But they make all the difference to a slightly apprehensive, somewhat puzzled adult who may be using the program for the first time. Similarly, professional programmers who are not educators may unwittingly assume considerable computer expertise in the learner, who may not understand what the various keys on the computer keyboard are for, or who can even be unfamiliar with a QWERTY layout in the first place. By suggesting ways of recognizing and resolving such problems, the SCEMP 'Guidelines' may prove useful for adult educators who want to co-operate with programmers in creating programs.

There are, of course, some much debated areas of 'good practice' in computer programming for adult learners that the 'Guidelines' leave unresolved. The matter of the best level of interaction between the learner and the program, for instance, is still very open for discussion. SCEMP recognizes that:

> The optimum level of interaction for new users is hard to define. Some users seem to be happier with the easy passive drilling of a program which just leads them straight through branching pages of text, by choosing options and pressing a key to continue. Others seem to prefer something more demanding, where they have to type in varied responses, which the computer then processes for them and returns results related to their responses in the form of a chart, a graph, a quiz score, or a rating. (SCEMP, 1982c)

Nor do the 'Guidelines' try to resolve the problem of how far computer programs for adults should aim to be as self-contained as possible and how far they should try to guide the learner to other educational media. Anyone who has had constantly to switch back and forth between perhaps half a dozen different types of material in an open learning course may very well feel occasional frustration at having to spend so much time on the media, rather than being able to give undivided attention to their messages. And computer programs, being a form of distance or open learning, can suffer from some of the same difficulties if they try to incorporate over-elaborate materials in addition to those provided on the computer itself. Indeed, the computer itself being so versatile and powerful, its programs can perhaps be more self-contained than material in many other open learning media. And, as we have already seen, computers can provide in many different ways for different kinds of learning experiences, so there may be less need to provide many other media. Clearly, however, computers remain only one way among others of enhancing adult learning, and any full learning experience will nearly always require that both people and other media are involved as well.

One final criterion which adult education may find helpful when they are helping to create computer programs is the need, clearly demonstrated recently by Paine (1983), to provide analogies to the hidden qualities of print as it is used in conventional learning. As Paine suggests, with print one can weigh up the size of the book or unit, flick through the pages to get a rough idea of content, style and approach, and easily mark those portions felt to be particularly important. These very characteristics are difficult to reproduce in many computer programs for adult learning, but analogies of them are essential and can be created by imaginative design.

Here, as elsewhere in the creation of computer programs, those learners for whom the material is designed will often be the best assessors of whether the programs really work. Sitting down with a new computer user at a learning program that one has until then thought foolproof is a chastening experience! Here too, as in the entire area of learning about computers (as we shall see in Chapters 4 and 6) both learners and tutors learn from one another.

The creation of good learning programs for adults is one of the most difficult problems that adult educators will have to face in trying to use the power and the flexibility of computers for adult learning. The specificity of computer programs tends to mean that it is simply not appropriate to adapt for adults most programs that have been written for children, quite aside from the rather different standards that apply to adult use. As the previous section has suggested, a number of good examples already exist, and more are being created all the time. But there is still a very long way to go before the full possibilities of the computer for adult learning are exploited to any significant extent.

But computer programs that are used directly by adults for their own learning are not the only ways in which adults may be said to learn with computers. Over the past few years there have also been a number of useful developments in computers that directly provide educational facilities to adults which they had not had before; any snapshot of learning with computers today will thus have to include a brief mention of the possibilities offered by Cyclops (the Open University's electronic overhead projector), computer-marked assignments (as used in the Open University and the National Extension College) and Telesoftware (the BBC's method of broadcasting computer programs which are then available for immediate use at home or in educational institutions).

Computers as Educational Equipment

Computer-linked equipment that enlarges the technological possibilities of how people communicate with one another continues to be widely developed and even more widely promoted by the developers. Much of it does not immediately seem relevant to the problems of adult learners, as we shall see in greater detail in Chapter 5 when we look at the kinds of information provided by computer-linked television services. But there have been three recent developments in equipment which do seem to offer help with quite specific problems in adult learning — the first by overcoming one important limitation of telephone tutorials, the second by virtually eliminating the need for long delays in getting feedback on assignments in correspondence courses, and the third by offering one possible way round the difficult problem of getting hold of good computer programs. None of the systems is yet widely used, but all of them offer sufficient possibilities for helping with these specific problems to merit at least a passing glance.

Adult learners who are geographically isolated from one another and from their tutor often find that telephone tutorials are one of the best substitutes for direct personal contact, and the Open University in particular has used such a method extensively with students in remote areas or on courses where the student population is very low and consequently scattered throughout the country. In a telephone tutorial both students and tutors can hear and be heard but they are, of course, unable to exchange any visual material: the kinds of concepts and illustrations that are often placed on a blackboard or an overhead projector in a conventional face-to-face session are simply impossible to present visually over an ordinary telephone.

In an attempt to enlarge the possibilities of telephone tutorials therefore, the Open University has developed a system known as CYCLOPS, which allows students and tutors to write and draw to each other by way of a television screen linked to a computer system and a telephone. The technical details and an evaluation of the system have been reported in a number of papers (including Sharples, 1982a and b; Sharples and McConnell, n.d.). The most striking result is that students preferred it to the alternatives of a long-distance journey to a study centre; the sheer convenience of the method thus rated highly.

But other factors were also present in the successful trials. Although it was used on courses from each of the six university faculties (arts, education, mathematics, social science, science and technology), the success of the system appeared to depend less on the content of the course than on the personality and conscientiousness of the tutor, who had generally to adopt a more constrained and directive style than normal.

Tutors themselves tended either to be very favourable or very unfavourable to the system: in one trial, four tutors dropped out because they felt CYCLOPS was incompatible with their teaching style, while the remaining eighteen recorded very favourable responses. The main uses which they made of the system were much the same as the main topics of Open University tutorials generally — going over core teaching material, teaching new material, going over tutor-marked assignments and academic problem solving. Here, as with many other uses of computers in adult learning, the equipment is useful for very specific purposes, but responses to it vary dramatically according to individual learning or teaching styles.

A second problem that often frustrates learners at a distance is the length of time that they often have to wait before finally receiving their marked assignments back from a tutor: a fortnight's delay is normal, and three or even four weeks is not uncommon where tutors are faced with numerous essays to be marked in addition to other academic commitments and family responsibilities. By the time one has waited for three weeks, ideas have become stale and of purely historical interest, as one has moved on to new material, sometimes misinterpreting it because of fundamental misunderstandings that one does not yet know about.

For many years the Open University has used a system of 'computer-marked assignments' to try to overcome this problem of delays in returning assignments. More recently, the National Extension College has developed a computerized system called 'MAIL' as a way not of replacing but of supplementing the feedback from distant tutors. The student sends in answers to as many as ten multiple-choice questions, and receives back within a few days a letter which replies to all of the answers with detailed comments on each, analysing any wrong choices and suggesting ways of reaching the right answer next time.

So far, the system has been used only in one NEC course, 'Make it Count', but the response has been very favourable indeed: virtually all of the learners who used this option completed the course (Freeman, 1983). There are, of course, serious constraints on how widely such a system could be used: it seems unlikely to be effective for long essays on the relationship between private and public life in *Middlemarch* or the treatment of marriage in *Anna Karenina*! Within these obvious limits, however, the computer-marked assignment does seem to have met a specific need and created a favourable response from nearly all the students who used it.

A third problem that often arises for adults who are using computers for learning at home is simply getting hold of good — or even just interesting — computer programs. As we have already seen, the general problem of providing substantial and or even merely useful educational programs for adult learners at a feasible price is one of the most formidable obstacles in the way of using computers in adult learning. There are a number of paths that adult educators might explore here, but the informal learner at home can already, if he or she has the appropriate computer and additional equipment, acquire programs free of charge from the BBC's Telesoftware service.

As this book goes to press, the service is only beginning, but the general shape seems fairly clear for the near future at least. The term 'Telesoftware' refers to the transmission of computer programs by broadcasting, or by cable, in a form in which they can be used by a computer at home (analogous, perhaps, to tape-recording a radio broadcast that one wants to hear later). In Telesoftware, the BBC plans to broadcast three types of programs which all have educational or at least educative potential. In the first place, they plan to transmit free-standing programs for general educational, domestic or entertainment purposes; programs to help computer users program more easily will be included. Secondly, they hope to broadcast programs that will support specifically educational broadcasts, and thirdly, programs that will enable learners to use the factual information that is available on Ceefax (the BBC's teletext service). Details of all programs available and times of broadcasting will be available on Ceefax.

Telesoftware will by no means in itself resolve the problem of finding good educational programs for adults. Among other constraints, its primary audience in the beginning is the many schools which now have BBC Computers. But the idea of public service broadcasting that includes computer programs amongst the material that it supplies, without charge to those who have the equipment to receive it, is clearly one important step in the direction of making more programs available to adult learners.

While there remains more problems than resolutions in the field of adults learning with computers, then, there are some difficulties that can be ameliorated by equipment that is already in use. Work with CYCLOPS, MAIL and Telesoftware may be said to enlarge the interesting possibilities that we have already considered in using computers for individualized instruction, discovery and unhampered learning. But the problems are formidable: much is going on, but there is often little serious evaluation of it and there are many unanswered questions.

Rather than close with a vision of the educational paradise that awaits all true lovers of computers, the last part of this chapter will try to sketch the work that remains to be done if adults are to be offered experiences with computers that will enrich their learning.

Research into Computers and Adult Learning

The questions that remain to be answered by serious research into the uses of computers for adult learning are nearly all of the questions one would wish to ask about the interaction generally between people and computers. In other words, we know very little, and very few attempts are being made to lighten the darkness of our ignorance. As Sage and Smith (1983) note, there is already a 'great wealth of expertise about the new technologies in education, but the bulk of it is not supported by a systematic information base . . . or by any depth of theoretical understanding'.

There are a number of possible reasons for such a paucity of research into the educational impact of computers. In the first place, there are obvious difficulties in conducting any prolonged research in a field, such as computer education, where both equipment and programs are still developing dramatically, and where much of the work is so specific that generalizations might be unsustainable.

Secondly, there are still such difficulties in clearing the way for adults to use computers that research into the educational effectiveness of any particular system or program would be a hazardous affair. As Lockwood and Cooper (1980) note, 'it is exceptionally difficult to evaluate the educational effectiveness of computer assisted learning in any obviously objective manner. There are almost always too many confounding factors to permit reliance in [sic] traditional methods.'

Finally, there is the question of what would constitute an acceptable form of educational evaluation of a computer program for adults. In what ways could one say, for instance, that a program to help people to stop smoking was 'effective'? It would be a relatively straightforward matter to point to ways in which it was useless if, for instance, the program kept breaking down so no one could actually use it, or if its messages were simply incomprehensible to most learners. But the measure of its effectiveness is a more complex and controversial matter (see Hawkridge, 1983a, and Hooper, 1977, for an introduction to the kinds of problems involved, which are also dealt with in Scanlon *et al.*, 1982 among many others). Some researchers also express serious doubt about the possibility or relevance of conducting research into computers which are used for learning in our current environments, where we often use computers to teach skills that the computers themselves have almost rendered irrelevant (see, for instance, Papert, 1980).

Despite these problems, there remains one outstanding fact that the limited research that has been conducted seems to support. When the equipment is working properly and when the programs have been devised with at least some awareness of their educational needs, many adults actively like using computers for learning. Lockwood and Cooper, 1980, for instance, report that they have 'canvassed a large body of information on student opinions regarding the use of computer assisted learning. If one may disregard the unfavourable comment that stems from machine and operational difficulties, reaction to the system has been almost wholly favourable.' They argue that 'student comment concerning the system and whether students continue in its use, are strong indicators of worth'. These positive indicators, as we have seen throughout this chapter, certainly seem to be present in every study so far carried out in the impact of computers on adult learning. The potential is clearly there.

But the questions that remain are far from trivial, as the range of issues already noted implies. There are serious social issues: depending on the context in which they are introduced, computers may be inaccessible to certain groups, including women and older people; and over-emphasis on individualized learning can seriously isolate people from one another. There are economic issues: there is the vexed matter of whether the use of computers for learning is ever 'cost-effective', although most recent commentators conclude that it probably is not (see Hawkridge, 1983a); and there is the further problem that if the individuals who use them are made to bear their full cost, computers and their educational programs will remain financially out of reach to many people.

The educational issues to be resolved are also both numerous and problematic. One wants, for instance, to ask how far the use of the technology itself shapes the messages perceived by the learners and whether the use of computers tends to create a sense of machine dependence in learning. The role of the educator as tutor also may need re-thinking in the light of the kinds of knowledge and information that can increasingly be provided by computer systems. So far the evidence seems to favour the conclusion that learning with computers is most likely to be satisfying when it is accompanied by human support (see, for instance, SCEMP, 1982b), but we have also seen that some people prefer the anonymity of the computer to contact with other people.

Very many questions about the general ways in which people respond to computers also require further investigation. There is already a significant body of work on the interaction of people and computers generally (summarized in Eason, 1982), but there is as yet little published evidence about the detailed expectations and satisfactions that adults experience with using computers for learning.

Investigations, in other words, have already barely begun, although researchers and postgraduate students are already showing an interest in the field of using computers for adult learning. But there are compelling reasons for not waiting until there is a significant body of evaluation and assessment before starting to offer adults the chances to learn with the computers that they seem to want. As we saw earlier in this chapter, there is already an expectation that computers are for adult learning, among other purposes, and many adults actively prefer to use them for certain kinds of education. As we have also seen in this chapter, computers for learning do go some way towards answering some specific problems in adult education, even if their power and versatility are only starting to be explored.

Finally, becoming familiar with computers through learning with them is an important step towards attaining a computer literacy which will enable us to try to control this power for our own ends, rather than make us feel alienated by it. As we saw in Chapter 2, computers are both potentially threatening and potentially liberating. It will only be when adults come to feel at ease with them that we can start to shape them to our own purposes. Learning with computers is one way of moving in this important direction, but as we shall now see in Chapter 4, there are many other ways in which adult education can also contribute to the spread of computer literacy.

4

Learning about Computers

What is the impact of the computer . . . on human dignity?
(Weizenbaum, 1976)

As Chapter 3 has tried to show, the power and the diversity of the computer make it a potentially significant tool for adult learning, and there are a number of imaginative and selectively useful ways in which adult educators are already experimenting with it. But, as Chapter 2 suggested earlier, the implications of computers range far beyond its educational uses.

It is because of these wider economic, political and social implications that — perhaps uniquely amongst the tools of the educator — the computer also demands attention as an object of study in itself. Indeed, its potential for both good and evil is so enormous that, even if they may choose not to apply it in their own work, adult educators will nevertheless have to take account of its impact. It may very well be that here lies the real significance of computers in adult learning.

Certainly during the next few years, a major challenge for adult educators will be the attempt to achieve national computer literacy: 'providing access to computer literacy is both in the mainstream of the liberal adult education tradition and a major challenge for its future' (Bostock and Seifert, 1983a).

The overwhelming need for computer literacy has already been implied throughout Chapters 1 and 2. As Chapter 1 argued, the ubiquitous presence of computers in the ordinary transactions of our lives and the extent to which children — often unlike their parents — seem to be entirely at home with them mean that adult educators need at least to take account of computers as one important factor in our world.

The case for computer literacy is further strengthened by the fact that the subject already has a substantial pool of potential learners. As Chapter 1 suggested, there is considerable public interest in the field: 'the amount of interest shown in computer applications cannot be stressed too much' (BBC, 1981). The very large responses to the BBC's Computer Literacy Project, to computing courses, and to public computer exhibitions are all evidence of substantial public enthusiasm for at least being introduced to the subject of computers.

The major case for working towards national computer literacy rests on the widespread effects and implications of the increasing computerization of our society. There are broadly three possible responses to these developments in computers. The first is a Canute-like attempt to turn back the tide of computerization which seems, certainly without a radical reorganization of our society, doomed to failure because of the sheer force of the economic, military and technological pressures that lies behind the drive towards computerization.

Probably the most prevalent response is the second one of technological determinism. Even in the world of education one sometimes uncovers a pronounced belief in the computer as a solution for which there ought to be a problem. This faith is clearly dominant in other areas in which computers are being applied, and there is often a sense that if it is technologically possible it ought to be done. An important article of this faith is the imposition of the standards of the computer technologists on the people who actually use their machines. Thus, human needs and preferences have to be adapted to the often unnecessary rigidity of many computer systems.

A third response is to recognize that 'technical imperatives define only what is possible, not what is *necessary*; what *can* be done, not what *must* be done' (Noble, 1981). As Laver (1980) sees it,

> computers are not the only, nor are they necessarily the most troublesome, of the new technologies that will affect our daily lives. However, the economic, social and political decisions which our use of them will require us to take are too important to be taken in ignorance, nor can they safely be left to experts — of whatever kind.

In any case, 'experts' are very likely to offer technologically biased answers to our problems, and offering the decisions to them would merely reinforce the tendency towards technological determinism. If we are to insist on our right to participate in decisions about what is actually done with computers, however, it is essential that we make such decisions on a well-informed basis. It is on the need for this third response that the real case for national computer literacy rests.

While the case for working towards national computer literacy may be easily made, one then has to ask what exactly 'computer literacy' consists of and how it might be achieved. These questions, which are rather more complicated to answer, form the basis of the rest of this chapter.

The Idea of 'Computer Literacy'

Earlier chapters have noted the widespread contact with computers that we now have in our daily lives. An extensive survey carried out by the BBC's Daily Survey of Listening and Viewing in 1981 showed that even then, of the four and a half thousand people interviewed from a representative sample of the adult public, nearly all had come into contact with computers either by using them at automatic cash-dispensers at banks or by seeing them in use at

Adult educators and computer literacy.

check-out points in shops (BBC, 1981). As computerization has spread even more widely since 1981, one can reasonably suppose that virtually everyone in Britain today has already had contact with computers in some form or other.

But this kind of casual acquaintance is clearly inadequate as a basis for making any kind of serious judgements about computers, apart from, perhaps the instant decision that one doesn't like a system that prints out the information that one has insufficient funds to make a withdrawal! On the other hand, it would be unrealistic to insist that judgements can be left only to those who are intimate with computers. Clearly, we need to identify some relationship between people and computers that lies somewhere between mere nodding acquaintance and the total knowledge and familiarity that comes with intimacy.

This middle ground between acquaintance and intimacy has come to be widely known as 'computer literacy'. In some respects the term is a helpful one, but there have been often greatly varying definitions of its meaning and, I believe, there are serious limitations in the implied analogy between print literacy and computer literacy.

The most vexed question is whether computer literacy actually includes being able to program computers. Unquestionably, there are important ways in which our everyday learning and thinking can be enhanced by familiarity with certain principles which are essential in computer programming. As Bostock and Seifert (1983a) note:

> As in the case of print literacy the use of the computer medium rubs off or spills over into ways of thinking, learning and experiencing. For example, the strategy of problem solving by dividing a problem into its smaller and more manageable components used in programming (top-down) can be applied with success to many areas. Other logical techniques such as repetition and recursion, characteristic of computer functioning will become integrated into cultural life as computer literacy spreads. Another example is that of the mistake and its treatment. The notion of error in traditional learning situations is treated in a negative way as a mistake to be ashamed of and avoided. (Correction of text on paper is messy, but in a computer medium it is simple and fast.) Computer programming treats errors ('bugs') as a normal part of the constructive process, and debugging as a necessary and positive activity. . . . Computer literacy . . . can thus add new ways of thinking to our normal cognitive processes.

It is with some justification, then, that many educators tend to assume that computer literacy will include at least a limited ability to program. Thus, the BBC's Computer Literacy Project includes an introduction to basic principles and practices of programming in its second series, *Making the Most of the Micro*, and the NEC courses on computer programming in BASIC are seen as an integral part of the process of becoming computer literate. At local level, most of the courses offered in computing for adult learners emphasize programming or the practical application of computers rather than public awareness (Taylor, 1983, and Gartside, 1982).

Certainly, the idea of print literacy has traditionally included not only the ability to read but also the ability to write. One can therefore argue, by analogy, that computer literacy should include the ability to 'read', to use other people's programs, and the ability to 'write', to create one's own programs. Thus, for instance, Radcliffe (1983b) holds that 'the route to computer literacy is through 'hands-on' experience. Some of this may be through ready-made programs, and some through do-it-yourself programming.'

The situation may, however, not be quite so straightforward as the analogy with print literacy makes it seem. It may be that so much emphasis has been placed on computer programming as a form of computer literacy because programming is what can be most easily provided. As Taylor (1983) suggests,

> the bulk of the provision . . . is geared to the practical application of microcomputers with only a minority of courses aimed at raising the general public awareness of the socio-economic effects of microelectronic developments. . . . But it seems too early yet to accept that the supply of courses is fully responsive to the demand.

In at least some of the institutions offering the many varieties of computer literacy, it may be that the choice of computer programming reflects what the institution can offer at least as much as public need or demand. As we saw earlier, there are as yet few educators who might feel qualified to teach a wider form of computer literacy, although there are increasing numbers of qualified computer programmers.

It is at least possible, then, that the current assumption that computer literacy must include computer programming stems partly from the fact that of all the elements that might be included in the concept, computer programming seems to be the most readily available. Paradoxically, it seems to me that this most widely available element is perhaps the least essential.

My case rests in part on Weizenbaum's (1976) question about the impact of the computer on human dignity. If one believes that the major reason for computer literacy is to enable people to make informed decisions about the human implications of computerization, computer literacy will have to include 'comprehension of and the ability to discusss computing concepts, applications and issues intelligently' (Bostock and Seifert, 1983a). However, to insist that people must also be able to implement their ideas about computers practically is perhaps analogous to arguing that one must be a car designer and a mechanic before being allowed to drive. In other words, such an attitude will tend to exclude most adults from participating intelligently in both discussion and decisions about computerization.

If computer literacy is not necessarily about the ability to program, of what might it consist? There seem to be three broad strands involved. First, computer literacy should mean being able to recognize in a general way both the usefulness and the limitations of computers. Secondly, someone who is computer-literate should be able to learn readily how to use computer programs. Thirdly, being computer-literate means being sufficiently aware of the ways in which computers are being used and can be used, so that one can make reasonably informed judgements about their effects. Above all, 'true computer literacy is not just knowing how to make use of computers and computational ideas. It is knowing when it is appropriate to do so' (Papert, 1980).

What, practically, does it mean to be able to recognize the usefulness and the limitations of computers? It does not mean knowing a great deal about the electronics of computers, but it would include, for instance, a general understanding of the binary principle on which most computers operate. It would include an appreciation of both the power and the diversity of computers, and some idea of what the differences in the capacities of computers mean for practical purposes. Someone who is computer-literate would not expect that any one computer could ever answer all of his or her computing needs, nor would such a person expect a microcomputer to perform as quickly and as powerfully as a larger machine. It might seem that such understanding is self evident, but certainly during the years in which the Scottish Community Education Microelectronics Project has operated, more than a few enquirers seemed to believe that they could store and quickly retrieve an enormous amount of information on the relatively small capacity of the SCEMP microcomputers.

The second element of computer literacy means being able to use a computer readily for one's own purposes — usually short of actually programming it. It will include basic familiarity with a computer keyboard: that is, being able to use the still-standard QWERTY arrangement of keys (as on an ordinary typewriter) and the most frequently needed of the additional computer keys which serve special functions.

The level of skill needed, as has already been noted, is far below that of a good typist, as computers themselves eliminate the need for conventional typing skills. For most practical purposes, it is sufficient merely to be aware of the fact that computers contain special keys and to know how to use a very few of them, such as the 'return' key and the keys that enable one to correct typing errors quickly and easily. This is the level of computer literacy for which limited practical experience of a computer of some sort is essential.

Both of these levels of computer literacy are a necessary but not sufficient condition for the third stage. It is here that, aware of the ways in which computers are being used, one becomes able to make informed judgements about their effects and implications. Here again the level of understanding required falls far short of being an expert. We do not need to know a great deal about computers to be able to see, for instance, that computerization can be socially divisive, even if only because sophisticated computer systems cost significant amounts of money. The real fears that exist about the computer society are pressing ones; only the computer literate will be able to deal with them in an informed way.

If we accept that these are three essential forms of computer literacy, we then need to look at how adult educators might contribute towards their realization. A large and growing amount of practical experience in offering public computer literacy is already available in Britain, and in the following discussion of some possible paths toward computer literacy I shall draw heavily on the experience which has been gained in computer exhibitions, courses and open learning materials.

Paths towards Computer Literacy: (1) *Exhibitions*

One of the most immediately attractive ways of providing computer literacy is to mount computer exhibitions for the general public. Of course, there are regular public computer exhibitions provided by those who have a commercial interest in persuading the public to use computers. Since 1982 there has also been a series of computer exhibitions in Scotland designed to interest and educate rather than to persuade people to buy. These 'Computers for All' exhibitions, mounted by the Scottish Community Education Microelectronics Project, have both raised and sometimes answered important questions about people's interaction with computers within the context of community education. No firm conclusions about their value can yet be drawn, as research on them is still incomplete as this book goes to press. But the experience so far suggests that this may be one important path towards greater computer literacy.

The main purpose of the 'Computers for All' exhibitions is to 'provide a gentle introduction to computers in a way that is not available anywhere else' (SCEMP, 1983). As the most recent report on the exhibitions points out:

> Some people consider that the role of the exhibitions is now being filled by leisure classes in computer studies, by department stores selling home computers, by computer clubs and computer camps. In fact, these organizations attract people who are interested in, and already motivated to learn about, computers. Many people are not so inclined. They are aware of the pressure to introduce computers created by the government, the commercial organizations and the media. Any nervousness about this pressure is aggravated by the stories from their children's schools about courses in Computer Studies. . . . For many people, this pressure, and a secret fear that the computer is a magic box only for the initiated, makes them unwilling to display their ignorance about computers or seek help. (SCEMP, 1983).

Between April, 1982 and August, 1983, SCEMP mounted eight major and many more minor public computer exhibitions throughout Scotland, in locations that included sports centres, libraries, pubs, voluntary organizations, health centres, theatres, conferences and shops. The exhibitions themselves have allowed people actually to use computers for a variety of educational and educative purposes. The computer programs available have included those which have already been discussed in Chapter 3 as well as several others of the same kind.

The most striking characteristic of the exhibitions appears to be the enthusiasm with which they have been welcomed by people who have never used computers before. While few precise figures are available, the evidence from those organizations which have hosted the exhibitions is that 'the machines have been fully occupied for most of the time that they have been available to the public' (SCEMP, 1982b), while in most locations there have been frequent queues behind the users, with crowd conditions prevailing at peak times. Where figures were available, they showed that the vast majority of the large numbers of visitors to the exhibitions had not previously used computers directly: 'more than 90 per cent of the 6,000 visitors to the Fife exhibition were first-time users' (SCEMP, 1983).

Responses to the exhibitions have so far shown marked variations depending on age and, to some extent, on sex .

> Differences in response according to age were noted by all observers. Staff present at the exhibitions noticed that young people never require any encouragement to use the computers, while the older members of their families often needed reassurance and positive encouragement. (SCEMP, 1982b).

Overall, men of almost all ages appeared to be more willing than women to use the computers, although this difference was never as dramatic as that usually implied by the sexual bias of most presentations of computers. Over the age of about sixty, both men and women appeared to be particularly reluctant to take part in any way (SCEMP, 1982b).

Other interesting findings from 'Computers for All' include apparent confirmation of the suggestion that adults seek very different paths to computer literacy. On the one hand, 'Aberdeen Library noted that, while there was a great interest in the exhibitions at the time, there have been few enquiries about follow-on activities. This would confirm that an interest in computers for many people extends no further than a simple hands-on experience' (SCEMP, 1983). On the other hand, 'the limited evidence available does suggest that the interest generated by the exhibitions may have resulted in an increased local demand for courses in computing' (SCEMP, 1982b).

Much the same phenomenon of wide initial public interest in computers combined with a much smaller persistent curiosity has emerged in the BBC's Computer Literacy Project (see Radcliffe and Salkeld, 1983) and elsewhere. This general pattern clearly has implications for how adult educators may try to fulfil the widely varying needs in this field, as I shall consider later.

Meanwhile, 'Computers for All' has established certain useful conditions for the success of public educational and educative exhibitions of computers (SCEMP, 1982b). First, the time spent in preparing for such an exhibition is probably much greater than for most public displays, because of the technical problems that arise both before and during the exhibitions, the need to prepare for the eagerness with which young people will monopolize the computers, and the creation of adequate educational support.

Secondly, it is essential that the sites should be staffed at all times by people who can answer the many questions that arise, maintain the machines and programs in good working order, discourage over-eager visitors from monopolizing the computers, and help the many visiting groups who will need formal introductions to the computers. In general, SCEMP found that the most frequent volunteers to help with the sites were young people but that the presence of adult staff was one important way of encouraging other adults actually to try the programs on the machines.

Finally, SCEMP found that it was important to provide for other ways in which people could satisfy their curiosity about computers other than by actually using the machines. Simply, there were never enough computers available to satisfy public demand. The exhibitions therefore provided a variety of other educational media, although none of these even remotely approached the computers in the ability to attract people. Indeed, perhaps the most important condition of success was that one should never underestimate the power of a computer!

Paths towards Computer Literacy: (2) *Courses*

As Taylor (1983) notes, 'there are many financial and organizational constraints on the adult education sector which make it enormously difficult to undertake any kind of new and innovative provisions'. The recent growth in courses about computers for adult learners is therefore particularly striking. As Chapter 1 has shown, over a single year the provision of courses in computing for adults almost doubled within local authorities and university extramural departments; the Workers Educational Association, too, considerably increased its provision (ibid). Even so, 'there seems to be scope for much more provision and no doubt there is much more demand which still remains unexpressed' (ibid).

There is ample evidence, then, that such courses are in great demand. But what exactly is the demand for? Here the answers are much foggier. The reasons that adults give for being interested in computer courses are enormously varied. Banks (1983), for instance, found a wide range of responses to his question about reasons for being interested in computers. They included: using the computer as an educational device for the family; to keep up with modern technology; for potential use at work; interest in purchasing a microcomputer; interest in the home-based office; concern about unemployment created by computerization; concern about access to computer information; interest in the effects of computers on education; for future use in a family business; and to broaden one's outlook.

Gartside (1982) uncovered much the same picture in his study of adult computer courses in Scotland. Participants in one course that he examined included: 'a gentleman of 62 wishing to keep up with his son at university, a farmer keen to know the best programmes to help with the operation of his farm, unemployed people . . . , hobbyists'.

The BBC also discovered at least two potential audiences for learning about computers. They found a committed, knowledgeable audience, such as people who regularly read computer magazines or who were professionally interested in the subject. But they also found a wider, more general audience, who were 'anxious about their capacity to understand the subject. The approach demanded by the more motivated section of the audience would almost certainly alienate them' (Radcliffe and Salkeld, 1983).

Computer courses, then, should be an example of the pluralism of adult learning in practice. But how far are the diverse aims of their participants realized in the courses themselves? Banks (1983) graphically describes the present difficulty:

> The audience is fluid and lacks clarity about exactly what it expects from educational efforts. Students do not have sufficient knowledge about the range of subject matter contained within the scope of the word 'computing' to be able to specify that their particular needs are in the area of programming skills, thinking skills, advice about careers or even a diffuse generalized interest in a new subject for the sake of the subject alone. It is a simple matter for the adult education system to provide large numbers of introductory computing classes, concentrating on program writing in BASIC, but if this does not meet the — admittedly often unrecognized — needs or wants of the students, then it is doing the students a disservice.

It may very well be that this discrepancy between the diverse needs of the adult learners and the relative uniformity of provision is one of the sources of the highly variable rate at which adult students have persisted in computing courses. In some of the courses studied by Gartside (1982), retention rates were very high indeed, ranging from 83 per cent to over 93 per cent. On the other hand, the completion rate for the NEC courses in BASIC has been one of the lowest in the history of the College (Freeman, 1983), and I personally know of more than one introductory computer course completed by fewer than 25 per cent of its enrolled students.

Chapter 3 has already emphasized the extent to which computers are likely to have a number of specific effects rather than necessarily any one general effect on adult learning, at least in the near future. The same phenomenon of extreme specificity seems to be occuring in the learning needs felt by adults who come to computers. Just as the pluralism of adults' learning needs requires many different approaches in learning by computer, so also learning about computers may need to branch from a general core to highly specific aims. It is notable, for instance, that one of the successful computer courses described by Gartside (1982) changed 'from initial aims which were course based to specific objectives based on the needs and wishes of the students'.

As Banks (1983) sees it,

> One answer may be to view introductory computing classes as a place where students can be acquainted with a whole range of issues within the panorama of computers and computing, so that they can focus their generalized interest into a discrete area which has relevance to themselves. Stemming from this 'sampler' core, perhaps it is possible to generate a whole compass of courses/packages, each package being tailored to a specific audience and being pro-

vided by the most effective media.

In computing courses for adults, however, the highly specific needs of the audience are not the only potential headache. There is also the major difficulty, which has emerged already in previous chapters and which will be tackled again in Chapter 6, that there are few adult educators who are already qualified to teach such courses and few computer experts who are skilled in teaching adults. In Scotland, the Scottish Community Education Microelectronics Project, caught in such a dilemma, sought the help of both an adult educator and a computer specialist. It may be that at least for the short-term future providers of computer courses for adults will find this a useful model.

Paths towards Computer Literacy: (3) *Open Learning*

In the broadest sense, computers themselves as a form of open or distance learning can provide one of the most useful ways of helping adults to learn about them, as Chapter 3 has already suggested. Anyone who has had much experience at all with computers will certainly be aware of at least some of their limitations! But as SCEMP's 'Computers for All' exhibitions discovered, using computers as a medium to discover more about computers often requires the presence of at least one human being who can mediate where necessary between people and machines. Despite the apparent logic of not using the methods of one medium to teach another, it may be that the computer by itself is not the ideal medium to teach about computers, although as we have already seen, practical experience of computers is one important part of computer literacy.

In this context it is significant that the major educational innovation in the field of open learning about computers for adults — the BBC's Computer Literacy Project — makes use of many paths towards computer literacy. The chief aim of this extensive and highly integrated project

> has been to introduce interested adults and younger students to the world of computers and computing. The project has been built around two ten-part television series, *The Computer Programme* and *Making the Most of the Micro*, and *The Computer Book*, an introductory course in programming provided by the NEC, a referral service, the BBC Microcomputer System and a range of applications software. Further series, courses, and software are planned and in preparation. (Radcliffe, 1983b).

These will include, in 1983/84, television series in the fields of data-processing ('The Electronic Office') and computer control ('Computers in Control') as well as a radio programme, 'The Chip Shop', aimed at both non-experts and the growing band of computer hobbyists; looking further ahead, there are preliminary plans for future series on the computer as a learning machine and on the social implications of computers (Radcliffe, 1983a).

The BBC path towards computer literacy.

Meanwhile, the Computer Literacy Project so far has been a dramatic success. There are, I think, many reasons for this success, and there are a number of important implications that the project already seems to have for adult education.

The first important characteristic of the BBC approach is its attempt to start with a series of the widest possible interest, and then to branch out into a variety of possibilities for further learning, using many different media to do so, including both computers and people. It has thus taken account of the highly specific and multiple needs of potential learners. Based as it was on detailed preliminary studies of the potential audience and the kinds of programs and learning materials in which they expressed serious interest, this approach clearly provides one very useful model for other adult educators.

Secondly, the introductory programme in the project, *The Computer Programme*, started not with the machine itself as seen by experts but rather with the point of view of a presenter who appeared to be new to the subject and who asked of the expert the kinds of questions that most newcomers would like to have professionally but simply answered. Throughout, the approach was 'designed to illustrate and explain the fundamentals of computing at both a practical and theoretical level, to be accessible to absolute beginners, and to encourage the audience to go further into the subject through the various other elements of the project' (Radcliffe, 1983b). Clearly, starting from the learner's rather than the expert's viewpoint was another reason for the success of the series.

A third element in the success of the television programmes has been the appeal across the barriers of sex, age and class that have characterized most computer applications. The first of the series, *The Computer Programme*, tended to attract rather more male than female viewers: females represented only 47 per cent of viewers despite forming 52 per cent of the population of the United Kingdom who are over 16 (Radcliffe and Salkeld, 1983). Even here the bias towards males was relatively small, at least compared with the usual ratio in other material about computers, where it is about ten males to every one female. In the second series, *Making the Most of the Micro*, however, the bias virtually disappeared, with the viewers being evenly divided between male and female (ibid).

Age as a barrier to participation in learning about computers has been noted in most experiments designed to introduce people to computers; SCEMP (1982b) found, for instance, that people over the age of 65 very rarely tried to use the computers in its public exhibitions. It is thus a promising result that, as Radcliffe and Salkeld (1983) note, those aged 55 and over formed as much as 24 per cent of the audiences for *The Computer Programme* and *Making the Most of the Micro* (34 per cent of the population of the United Kingdom are over 55).

The question of the extent to which different social classes participate in adult learning is a vexed one that depends in part on one's definitions of adult learning. It is generally recognized that as one descends the social scale, participation in adult learning tends to decrease (see, for example, ACACE, 1982a). The viewing figures for the Monday late-night transmissions of both

BBC series are therefore particularly encouraging for those who believe that, carefully and sensitively used, computers can provide access to learning for people who might otherwise not be attracted to it.

Middle-class social groups tended to watch BBC series in approximately the same proportion as they are represented in the population as a whole: in the social class grouping used for the BBC, 35 per cent of the population of the United Kingdom are considered to be middle class, and 34 per cent of the audience for each series was classified in the same way. The really striking figures occur for those considered to be working class. In particular, members of the skilled working class watched both series in much larger numbers than one might have predicted: whereas this group forms about 33 per cent of the population of the United Kingdom, 42 per cent of the audience for *The Computer Programme* fell into this category. Even amongst the lowest social groups, the proportion of viewers was considerably higher than is normally the case for participation in adult learning: 26 per cent of the audience for *Making the Most of the Micro* was considered to come from the lowest social class groups, which comprise about 35 per cent of the population as a whole (Radcliffe and Salkeld, 1983).

At this stage one can only speculate on the possible reasons for this remarkable ability of both series to appeal across the traditional barriers of sex, age and social class. The television series clearly drew some of their success from the growing popular appeal of microcomputers, and from the creation and highly successful promotion of the BBC Computer itself. The sheer excellence of the programmes themselves, as may be seen in the substantial national and worldwide use of them (ibid), is a contributory factor.

But perhaps the major factor in the BBC's success has been the insistence on starting from where the learner is, rather than imposing the terms of the computer world itself. The programmes have emphasized the power and the diversity of computers, and have shown both sexes, all ages and people from many different occupations happily using them. And as we have already seen the overall project within which they have been transmitted has allowed people to look at *The Computer Programme* for a general introduction and then to follow up more specific interests in a wide variety of ways. Measured by its widespread acceptance, the formula has been unquestionably successful.

As Chapter 1 has already noted, the success rate for the other elements in the Computer Literacy Project has also been outstanding. The figures for popular responses to the project are, measured against comparable exercises, very impressive. Within the first eighteen months, there were about 200,000 enquiries to the computer referral service provided by Broadcasting Support Services, while about 120,000 copies of the NEC's three editions of the computer programming course in BASIC, which was linked to the project, had been sold by the spring of 1983 (ibid).

Here, however, a somewhat unexpected result emerges: enthusiastic enrolment in the correspondence courses in programming has been followed by a very low rate of completion of the courses (Freeman, 1983). As with the success of the television programmes, one can only speculate on the possible reasons. Obviously anyone who buys his or her own computer and tries to learn to program it will have a number of sources of learning already available, and will thus not be dependent on a single correspondence course; indeed, the computer itself can do more than a little of the teaching needed.

It is also possible, however, that the very nature of computer programming may make it particularly difficult for novices to learn by way of a correspondence course: the relentlessly logical nature of computer programming means that even a single error in a text can have disastrous consequences for the inexperienced learner. It is also possible that texts written by experienced programmers may easily, if unintentionally, presuppose a greater grasp of mathematical and logical principles and practices than many learners may have. Finally, the frustration often experienced by new computer owners, when their machines fail to live up to their inflated expectations, may also be a factor in the failure to complete a course in programming.

Overall, perhaps the major finding of the Computer Literacy Project so far has been its demonstration of 'a real underlying public demand' for learning about computers (Radcliffe and Salkeld, 1983). There is a large audience for computer literacy, and the BBC figures imply that even people who do not normally participate in adult learning may be attracted to the possibility of learning about computers. The way is thus wide open for adult educators to take advantage of the experience provided by the project and to explore new ways of acquiring computer literacy through open learning.

A Wider View of Computer Literacy

Each of the paths towards computer literacy can provide an important way for individuals to move more easily in the powerful and versatile world of computers. But the many issues involved in computerization are not susceptible to the kind of analysis that individuals on their own can give them. As Chapter 2 has shown, it is not individual familiarity or use but the economic, political and social contexts in which computers are applied that will finally determine their effect.

Those who care about adult learning will therefore want to look further than merely providing computer literacy for individuals. Indeed, it may be that true computer literacy will be achieved only when people acting in communities are able to use computers for their own purposes. Chapter 5 will therefore consider some of the ways in which voluntary organizations and groups have been trying to harness the power of computers for their communities.

5

Computers and Community Education

What life have you if you have not life together?
There is no life that is not in community.
(T. S. Eliot, 'Chorus II' from *The Rock*)

Since this book is about the relevance of computers to adult learning rather than about theories of adult or community education, I shall sidestep the awkward question of the differences or similarities of adult and community education. Since there was a calculated absence of any definition of adult learning in Chapter 1, the reader will scarcely be surprised at this later reluctance to say what, precisely, community education is.

For the purposes of this book, I am viewing community and adult education as two interlocking circles (parents whose children are doing set theory at school might think of them as a Venn diagram). Each concept includes elements not present in the other, but they also share important common interests in, for instance, the learning experiences created by voluntary organizations and the various forms of responsive education. In dealing with computers and community education, then, I am writing about matters that are intimately related to — but not identical with — adult learning.

The main reasons why computers and community education are of interest to adult educators do not lie, of course, in these laboured problems of definitions. As Chapter 4 suggested, using computers for the benefit of the wider community may very well be one major form of computer literacy. Moreover, as Chapter 2 suggested, the serious effects and implications of computerization mean that any use of computers to meet human needs rather than primarily for economic or military gain will matter to all those who care about adult learning and the context in which it takes place.

More specifically, there are a number of important ways in which computers can enable or support, rather than provide, adult learning. One obvious example is the provision of highly specific, individualized information about educational opportunities. Another way in which computers might be said to enable adult learning is in their use as communication aids for those who are so physically handicapped that they cannot take part in many conventional forms of learning. Also, where computers are used to ease or even remove

SCEMP Scottish Community Education Microelectronics Project

COMMUNITY PROGRAMS

Local Organisations **by Bishopbriggs High School**

This program enables you to build up a file of information about local organisations. The file can be revised easily, to add, change or delete information. A printout can be obtained of all or parts of the file.

An Introduction to Wordprocessing **by the Scottish Microelectronics Development Programme**

This program introduces the principles of wordprocessing in a very simple way. The package contains user notes with easy-to-follow instructions.

Sniffing Glue - and other solvents **by the Scottish Microelectronics Development Programme and The Greater Glasgow Health Board**

This program tries to survey the problem of solvent abuse and allows you to compare your attitude to it with the reactions of a group of teenagers.

Rise and Shine **by the Scottish Microelectronics Development Programme and The Scottish Health Education Group**

A program which helps you to realise that how you rise in the morning affects how you feel and your relationship with others for the rest of the day.

Managing Redundancy and Unemployment **by Scottish Adult Basic Education in collaboration with SCEMP**

This program contains information on many aspects of redundancy including tax, redundancy pay and what to do with it, how to use spare time and look for jobs. A number of sources for further information are also given.

Computer programs to serve diverse communities.

tedious tasks from administrators in educational or educative organizations, they may well be contributing, at least indirectly, to the support of adult learning.

The idea of using computers 'in the community' is so diffuse a concept as almost to be amorphous. The needs of any community are so numerous and so broad, while the functions that can be performed by computers are so specific, that at first glance there seems unlikely to be any good fit between computers and community needs. Chapter 3 sought first to draw attention to some current needs in adult learning and then to suggest how computers might help to meet these needs. Such an approach will obviously not work in discussing computers and communities.

I have therefore decided instead to consider three main areas in which computers directly or indirectly enhance adult learning within community education: their use for administrative purposes within voluntary organizations, their provision of social information and their development as communication aids for various kinds of physical disability. All of these areas raise inportant issues — particularly the need for human mediation and the problem that it is often difficult to translate initial enthusiasm for community computing into practical achievement. These issues, and ways of resolving them, will be considered in this chapter, and a number of ways in which communities can make use of the power and diversity of computers will be suggested. I shall also discuss the factors that community organizations may want to consider before moving ahead to computerize any of their services.

There will be no attempt to give a comprehensive view of the many different developments that now use computers for community education. Rather, using a few selected projects for illustration, I shall merely try to give a taste of the innovations currently under way.

The Computer as Work-horse

Whatever the consequences on unemployment, it is generally accepted that computers can improve the efficiency of much office work: 'advanced equipment . . . can replace many functions performed by clerks, typists and secretaries' (Werneke, 1983). It is thus not surprising that many organizations in adult and community education, which are often hard-pressed to carry out a multitude of tasks with insufficient staff, are attracted to the possibility of computerizing some of their office work.

The experience of the Scottish Community Education Microelectronics Project confirmed this widespread interest in using the computer simply as a work-horse. Although there had been no public announcement that SCEMP would lend computers to voluntary organizations, the numbers of requests for such loans in the early months of the project far exceeded the equipment available. Despite SCEMP's initial intention not to encourage use of the computers for such now conventional tasks as word processing and accounting, community organizations primarily wanted to use them in just such ways. Particularly where under-staffing is a chronic problem, there is an obvious attraction to anything which might ease the pressures on existing staff.

As we shall see later in this chapter, the assumption that a computer will immediately and permanently relieve the pressure created by shortage of staff is unjustified. Nevertheless, it is clear that if the system is well chosen and carefully used, computers can relieve the workload involved in administrative support. The creation and production of almost every kind of written document is much faster when one uses a computer to manipulate text; thus letters, official papers, agendas, minutes, information releases, press statements and all the other documents that emanate from voluntary organizations can be prepared more efficiently by using a good word processor. Maintaining membership lists, subscription files and so on can also be done more efficiently on an appropriate computer system.

Certain kinds of financial records can also be more efficiently maintained by computers, although it is still difficult to find commercially available packages that are fully suitable for many voluntary organizations: unlike commercial enterprises, most community organizations work on yearly grants rather than regular weekly or monthly incomes. But where there is a significant amount of financial management, computers can often save considerable time.

There are also other tedious and time-consuming tasks in community organizations which could be done much more efficiently by computerization. For instance, the creation of rotas of voluntary helpers, where many different people with many different requirements are involved, can be simplified by using a computer to do the sorting. Another example where computerization can save time is the maintaining and cross-referencing of long lists of learning resources and other printed materials.

The computer as an administrative work-horse therefore has many possible advantages for the work of community organizations in their indirect support of adult learning. There are, however, a number of important factors to take into account before moving towards computerization; these are considered later in this chapter.

Computers and Social Information

During the past few years in Britain there has been a growing amount of interest in the possibilities of using computers and allied telecommunication systems to provide what is known as 'social information'. The term 'social information' generally refers to the wide variety of information that people may need in their everyday lives, such as their entitlement to welfare benefits, information about careers and educational opportunities, advice about health, information about local community affairs and organizations, consumer advice and so on. One of the main features of such information is that it may very well not have direct commercial value, although its helpfulness to individuals and groups may be considerable.

So far the main kinds of social information explored by computer projects have been entitlement to welfare benefits, information about educational opportunities and careers advice. There have also been a number of experimental projects to provide public information about local communities. In addition to these specific forms of social information, there have been several investigations of the more general social information provided by Prestel (the computerized British Telecom system that provides information by way of a television screen linked to a telephone).

Computers and Social Information: (1) *Welfare Benefits*

At first glance, there are many potential advantages in offering people a chance to determine their entitlement to welfare benefits by way of a computerized system: the combination of a large amount of detailed information about state benefits, specific information about individual circumstances and rapid calculation of individual entitlement make a computer seem ideally suited to the task. The two major microcomputer systems which have been developed so far help people in this way are the 'Cardiff' system, developed by the Cardiff Citizens Advice Bureau for use by staff, and the 'Surrey' system, developed at Surrey University for use directly by clients and currently being evaluated by the Department of Health and Social Security.

The idea behind each of these computer systems is that clients can receive precise advice about their likely entitlement to state benefits. At least in theory, the system intended for staff ought to save time in getting hold of the specific regulations applicable to each client and in calculating the entitlement of each client; the Cardiff system also provides a print-out of entitlement to benefit that can be taken to the local Social Security office to support claims. The Surrey system offers individual clients a chance to use the computer themselves to enter their personal circumstances and to receive an entirely private assessment of their entitlement.

So far, both systems have significant disadvantages in practice, and some commentators have been uneasy about what they perceive as theoretical disadvantages as well. As the information contained on each system has to be absolutely accurate and up to date, both systems need continuous up-dating. Moreover, social security regulations often require interpretation that no computer system could readily provide. An additional limitation so far is that many less widely used benefits are simply not included in the systems — as this book goes to press, strikers' pay, for instance, is omitted. Practically, the Cardiff system requires a considerable amount of staff training, which may create a problem for hard-pressed volunteers in a busy office. The Surrey system seems to be time-consuming to use, and may prove difficult to integrate with the work of human advisers.

Sheffield Computers for People (1983) have recently pointed to a number of theoretical disadvantages of such systems too. One difficulty is that

> many interviews between enquirer and advice worker may require much more than economic advice. It may be that more personal or political help is required, and a computer system may focus the interview too much towards a narrow definition of the problem. . . . The situation relies on the advisor knowing when *not* to use the system or when to give up.

A further possible danger is that 'benefit systems deal with the more common cases and exclude regulations concerning minority groups. . . . If an "efficient" . . . system is created for the mainstream . . . claimants, the service to minority groups is likely to get worse'(ibid).

Both of these theoretical difficulties appear to be problems that could be resolved by being aware of their possibility and then actively seeking to overcome them. There is nothing inherent in the systems themselves which compels such outcomes; the problems arise from how they are used by people.

Even given the practical problems that welfare benefit systems may now have, their potential for educating people about their entitlement to benefit must not be underestimated. At their weakest, such systems are valuable 'as an educative tool by which potential claimants can assess their own position before proceeding to personal interview with an adviser' (SCEMP, 1982b). They can also provide entirely impersonal and private information for someone who prefers not to speak immediately about his or her personal problems to a stranger. At best, such systems can offer more informed help to more people than could be provided by human means alone.

Computers and Social Information: (2) *Careers Advice*

Career advice is another area where there is an evident need to match complicated information to individual circumstances and preferences. Here a number of possibilities relevant to adult learning are being explored. They all generally require those seeking advice to complete fairly lengthy questionnaires about their preferences for work activities, their dislikes, the kinds of conditions they want to work under and the kinds of abilities they think they have. The answers are then analysed by the computer, which prints out a list of suggested occupations, sometimes ranked according to preference.

Studies of two of the systems currently used by adult learners suggest that students are using them 'to look at their self-perception and values' (Gibbons and Simpson, 1982; see also Wilson, 1983) as part of, not in place of, the process of consulting human advisers. The general response so far seems to be favourable. For many of the students in Gibbons and Simpson's study,

> to approach the computer seemed to be a much less threatening process then talking to a human being, at least initially. . . . You don't have to worry about your inadequacies, or the fact that you are taking up someone's valuable time. . . .

> Having taken the first step with a computer it looks as though people are much more able to take further steps with a human counsellor.

The use in the Extra-Mural Studies Department of Edinburgh University of a system intended initially for school-leavers but adapted for women returners has also had favourable responses. 'Both the Department and most of the women students have been satisfied with the operation of the new system which is not viewed as a replacement for careers guidance but as a useful adjunct to it' (Wilson, 1983). The advantages of using the system with a group of women of mixed ability include, Wilson says, the fact that for women who have been at home for some time, self-assessment is often very difficult by more conventional methods; students enjoy the process of providing information for the computers; and the best and the least qualified are all treated equally to a print-out of the same length, which provides a concrete point from which they can start to consider the qualities needed for different jobs.

Here, perhaps because the systems are intended to be used not in place of, but in conjunction with, human advice, both adult educators and students have been enthusiastic about computers that can enlarge and enhance careers advice. Such systems are still experimental, however, and none as yet is specifically designed to cope with the wide variety of experiences and expectations of adult learners. Nevertheless, the future seems promising.

Computers and Social Information: (3) *Educational Information*

The closely related area of information about educational opportunities for adults is also being affected by computerization. There have been a number of experimental pilot projects here, but the most substantial development is the new Educational Counselling and Credit Transfer Information Service, which is due to be available from January, 1984. Here, as with careers advice and welfare benefits entitlement, there are clear advantages in using a computerized system to try to match highly complex and extensive amounts of information to individual needs. ECCTIS, which is being developed by the Open University for the Department of Education and Science, 'aims to provide information on all the courses offered at Universities and polytechnics *throughout the UK*; and all the other courses in further education leading to qualifications, other than GCE, *throughout South West England*' (ECCTIS, 1983); the intention is eventually to cover further education throughout the country.

The need for such services is widely documented (see, for instance, Legge, 1981, and ACACE, 1982b), and was recognized as an important priority by both the Russell and the Alexander Reports. As ACACE (1982a) showed, one of the main reasons why adults did not follow a course they wished to do was simply that they did not know whether it was available. It is obvious that the computerized services which ECCTIS intends to provide will by no means meet all of the information needs of adults wishing to embark on learning:

among other restrictions, ECCTIS will include only courses in formal higher and further education.

Within these limitations, however, ECCTIS does aim to provide information about both the courses themselves and the level of qualifications which have been accepted for entry to them. Moreover, it is intended to be 'particularly useful for mature students entering or re-entering higher education, and for those seeking post-experience vocational courses for retraining or upgrading their knowledge' (Frogbrook, 1983). It thus represents a considerable advance in providing accurate and up-to-date information about educational opportunities for adults.

Quite aside from the fact that its information will be limited to certain kinds of courses, ECCTIS also raises two important issues in the field of providing computer-based information services for adults. The first of these is that the information will eventually have to be bought: once its initial grant has expired, it is intended that it should operate as a self-financing body (ECCTIS, 1983). The second issue is that the information which it will provide will often need to be interpreted for many enquirers by a knowledgeable counsellor or adviser; funds to pay for this kind of service are notoriously scant.

The nationwide service which ECCTIS is intended to provide will also clearly not answer enquiries about local non-formal and informal opportunities for adult learning. Here, information held on computers in community organizations could be helpful, and there have been a number of pilot projects to explore the possibilities of using the computer as a kind of 'sophisticated notice-board' (SCEMP, 1983).

The Scottish Community Education Microelectronics Project has undertaken several experiments in this area. The most substantial of these projects has involved a joint venture with Motherwell Library, where computerized information on over 800 clubs, societies and public services has been available for the general public since the spring of 1983. By the summer of 1983, the Library was handling about 40 enquiries a week from this service, 90 per cent of them from individuals (SCEMP, 1983). Because of the limited capacity of the computer system used, there are limitations on the ways that people can actually ask for the information: one cannot ask, for instance, 'what clubs are available on a Tuesday night or what societies have creche facilities' (ibid). Nevertheless, 'the number of requests for information has surprised even the Library . . . and has shown . . . that there is a demand for information of this kind from groups and individuals' (ibid).

The potential for further developments of this kind is obviously considerable, as a number of other developments throughout the United Kingdom are discovering. Libraries in particular have been enthusiastic about the possibilities of providing computerized information (see, for example, SCEMP, 1983, and Kania, 1983).

It may very well be that making such information available has no effect on the take-up of opportunities in community education — no one has yet proved that making the information available on a computer has any significant effect on the subsequent attitudes or behaviour of the enquirer. But the sheer public enthusiasm for the system at Motherwell and others like it strongly suggests that this an avenue worth exploring further in using computers for community education.

Computers and General Social Information

Computers, then, may be a valuable way of providing specific social information in particular contexts. What is the potential for community education of a more general system of public information such as that provided by British Telecom's Prestel?

One of the most far-reaching of recent experiments in using computers for community education has been the 'Prestel for People' project carried out in the period 1981–3 for the Social Information Providers' Group, through a grant from the Department of Industry. The project had three objectives:

> to define how social information on Prestel could best be developed to meet the needs of the domestic market; . . . to see whether it would be possible to link the development of the database to the sale of sets to organisations . . . [which] have a responsibility for providing the public with information and advice, especially in the public and non-profit sectors; . . . to increase the awareness of Prestel among the general public. (Kania, 1983).

The project set up Prestel sets in forty public sites and monitored the use made of them and the reactions of members of the public to this contact with new technology. The account which follows is based on the final report of this project (ibid).

The project assumed that 'social information' included information about education, best buys and consumer advice, local facilities such as clinics, solicitors and leisure centres, legal information about such things as divorce and consumer credit, employment and housing information and citizens' rights. People who used the sets by no means used them simply for these purposes; some of the main areas of interest were travel and entertainment.

While overall the public users generally expressed satisfaction, those who wanted serious social information were often disappointed. The greatest satisfaction seemed to be with information of a light general nature rather than with more specific detailed serious searches: for instance, while local information was widely sought, only 40 per cent were satisfied with what they received.

Three aspects of the overall findings are particularly relevant for the uses of computers in community education. In the first place, the computerized information provided by Prestel was felt to be useful by most of those who saw it, and the medium itself was enthusiastically received: 91 per cent of the users said they would come back to use it again. Here again is confirmation of how very acceptable computerized information may be to the general public.

Secondly, the most enthusiastic users were young male skilled workers, a further indication that computers may prove a particularly attractive medium for community education with this social group.

Thirdly, the project found that public libraries provided perhaps the most effective public access to Prestel; indeed, the report goes on to recommend that 'every encouragement should be given by local authorities to provide special funding for the placing of public access Prestel terminals in libraries.' Combined with the finding of enthusiastic public support for the computerized information services provided by certain SCEMP initiatives, this outcome of 'Prestel for People' clearly suggests that computerized library information services may be well worth developing further as an important contribution to community education.

There are therefore a number of recent indications that computerization of many forms of social information may be an attractive and effective way of reaching the general public. Several important issues remain to be discussed further (and will be considered later), but it does seem as if — at least when they are supported by human mediators — computers provide one of the most valuable and useful ways of giving social information.

Computers and Communication for the Disabled

Using computers in community education to be work-horses or to provide social information opens up new options for supporting adult learning. The possible use of computers as a communication aid for the disabled does much more than merely open up new options. In many cases, such a use of computers can make possible educational experiences that would not otherwise be available to people with certain kinds of disability.

Overall, the challenge that has to be met in this field is that, at present, 'most handicapped adults in Britain do not find the opportunities for education which they clearly want' (Mohr, 1977). The problem goes far beyond anything that computers might be able to ameliorate. However, there have been so many striking developments in using computers in this field that, despite the difficulties, there seems to be much promise for the future.

The whole field of computer-based aids for the disabled is now so developed that entire books are devoted to the subject (see, for instance, Perkins, 1983). My main concern here, however, is with those ways in which computers can provide access to learning for physically disabled adults, particularly by enlarging and enhancing the kinds of communication available to them. There are also important ways in which computers may contribute to learning for mentally handicapped individuals, but that topic needs specialized attention of a kind that I do not feel qualified to give.

As indicators of the kinds of developments currently taking place, I shall consider here two major physical disabilities which may directly inhibit communication and therefore may restrict certain kinds of learning: blindness and the inability to move most or all parts of the body. In both cases, computer-based aids can exploit the remaining abilities to make possible the kind of communication that will open up significant learning experiences.

The possibilities of communication to and from someone who is blind have increased dramatically over the past few years, although here, as elsewhere in the field of communication with those who are disabled, what is technologically feasible is often financially impossible. One of the major developments here has been the creation of reading machines and other uses of synthetic speech to enable people who are blind to hear material that originally existed in printed form (Perkins, 1983).

Other the significant advances include ways of making it possible for blind people to cope directly with computers, so that the information provided by a computer appears in the form of braille (Vincent, 1983). The Open University is also developing a number of ways of helping blind students to use computers as readily as people with sight, and to communicate in written form with as much ease as people who can use an ordinary typewriter. It is now possible, for instance, for a student to type an essay in braille, which will be converted to standard text for a sighted tutor to read (ibid).

For those who are unable to use most parts of their body to communicate, there has been a considerable amount of work on making it possible for them to use the power and the diversity of computers. As Odor (1982) notes, this work has concentrated on communicating with computers by bypassing the physical limitations from which the individual is suffering. The general idea is that computers can be specially programmed so that they can be used with a minimal amount of body movement. Someone who cannot use his or her hands for entering information on the keyboard of a standard computer, for instance, can instead use other ways of operating the computer by specialized devices. The kinds of devices used include specialized switches which can be operated by gross limb movement, grunt detectors, direct pick-up of muscle or nerve potentials, use of the voice where speech is unimpaired and detection of line of gaze, for those whose eye movements represent their only form of communication.

The major difficulties in the whole field of communication aids for the disabled now lie not so much in the ingenious creation of such devices to enhance communication but in making them available at a feasible cost. The problem is the very specificity of the communication and educational needs of any one disabled adult. The development of computer applications is highly dependent on there being either a mass market — for inexpensive applications — or a great deal of money available. Neither condition will apply to communication aids for the disabled. 'We are talking about products for a very small sector of the market overall: when we consider each intersection of educational function and communication aids, the potential number of customers is tiny indeed' (ibid). Moreover, each customer will need expensive support well beyond the capacity of conventional commercial suppliers.

Development in this field is therefore concentrating more and more on adapting commercially available computers by specially fitted additional equipment that makes it possible for someone who is disabled to use the machines (Perkins, 1983). More attention is also being paid to the circumstances in which disabled people are able to use computers most effectively. One of the loans made by the Scottish Community Education Microelectronics Project was to an organization that houses severely disabled adults, many of whom were spastic or had multiple sclerosis. The project found that the computers were enthusiastically welcomed, but that it was important to provide the disabled users with relative quiet; several short periods rather than one long one; freedom to work individually at their own speed; and programs that provided an immediate response to overcome possible lack of concentration (SCEMP, 1983).

There are therefore many ways in which computers can be used to enhance communication for people who are disabled, thereby opening for them the possibility of learning experiences which they would otherwise be cut off from or would have found particularly difficult to manage. Many of the technical possibilities, however, are unlikely to be realized unless community organizations offer the kind of information and support that only people can provide. Here again, human mediation is essential if computers are to enhance adult learning.

Computers and Counselling

Virtually all of the projects described in this chapter have raised, either explicitly or by implication, the question of whether computerized information and communication systems are most effective if directly presented to the public or whether it is better to provide a human mediator of some kind, often an adviser or counsellor.

This is highly controversial ground. On the one hand there are those who argue that to try to interpose a human interpreter between an enquirer and his or her information is to be patronizing and even potentially authoritarian. The 'Prestel for People' project, for instance, concluded that intermediaries to guide the public proved to be as much a deterrent as a help, and that in future developments the public should be allowed free direct access to the computerized information (Kania, 1983).

There is also considerable evidence from a variety of sources that many people prefer the anonymity of communicating with a computer to actually speaking with an adviser or counsellor. SCEMP has found that 'the public have recognized very quickly that computers can give them information of a sensitive nature without the embarrassment of an interview with a professional' (SCEMP, 1983). Much the same advantage was claimed for the use of computer-based careers advice for Open University students (Gibbons and Simpson, 1982) and for computerized calculation of entitlement to welfare benefits (Sheffield Computers for People, 1983).

A diametrically opposite stance is taken by those who wonder whether computers should have any place at all in advisory or counselling services or, indeed, in community education as a whole. 'There are those who would question the relevance of computers to a service which is about caring and counselling at an individual level' (McDonald, 1983b). I have heard many people who care about learning wondering aloud whether the introduction of any form of computerization will distort the human relationship between the enquirer and his or her counsellor.

The issue, it seems to me, yet again comes down to making an informed and sensitive judgement about those areas in community education for which computerization is appropriate. Just as computerization can cause unemployment or can improve the quality of work, depending on the context in which computers are introduced and the purposes for which they are used, so also computerized information and communication may enhance or deform the relationship between people that lies at the heart of community education.

There are some circumstances in which computerization appears to be the most attractive solution: some people prefer to use computers to elicit personal help, and sometimes a large amount of information has to be manipulated for highly individual needs. The real need now is for those who care about adult learning in whatever context to develop sufficient computer literacy to be able to determine when it is appropriate to use such high technology — and when it is not.

Deciding to Use Computers — or Not

For those who are considering whether computerization would be helpful for their own work in community education, there are a number of sources of practical advice, which are listed in Appendix 2. Meanwhile, some of the most important factors involved have been identified by the Scottish Community Education Microelectronics Project in its many loans of computers to community organizations, and it may be useful to consider briefly some of the lessons which SCEMP believes it has learned over its first two years.

The most common consideration in deciding whether to computerize is characteristically summed up as: 'There is some money available. Let's spend it on a computer and we will work out how to use it later' (McDonald, 1983c). The general reasons against this attitude are amply dealt with by Covvey and McAlister (1982). Within community education in particular, the result is often that a computer arrives in an office where the hard-pressed staff resent its intrusion, and where it is used at all it disrupts or distorts previously acceptable patterns of work.

Rather than start from the question of availability of spare money, SCEMP has found that a more fruitful approach is first to ask whether computerization is likely to be useful at all: 'a computer should be considered only if it can perform a task which has to be done more efficiently and accurately' (SCEMP,

1982b). Second, it is crucially important to determine exactly what functions the computer is initially needed for, whether they are compatible with one another and whether one can acquire suitable programs to perform them.

A third consideration is whether the capacity of the computer will be able to cope with the real volume of the information that one hopes to use it for: many affordable systems are simply too slow and too small to deal effectively with large amounts of information. Fourth, one needs to ask whether the computer will be used primarily by the staff or by the general public or both; where it is primarily for staff use, there will be the serious issues of staff reactions and training to consider.

Finally, there are practical details such as where the computer will be placed, how it will affect work patterns, what kind of security arrangements can be made and what kind of scheme can be agreed for repairs. For each of these decisions, informed professional advice is at least helpful and may often be essential.

Meanwhile, it may help to note SCEMP's straightforward list of *do's* and *dont's* about introducing computer systems into community organizations:

> *Do* have well-defined objectives within the capabilities of the machine and the programs that are available.
> *Don't* try to tackle too much and end up achieving little.
> *Do* identify a progression of steps, leading to objectives, which will be within the staff's computer experience at the time.
> *Don't* raise expectations of early success. Disappointments are difficult to erase from people's memories.
> *Do* ensure that there is staff available to support the investment in equipment.
> *Don't* expect a computer to ease workloads initially.
> *Do* involve all members of staff in any changes.
> *Don't* allow an elite of computer-literates to emerge.
> *Do* match the calibre of the staff to the task.
> *Don't* abandon traditional methods until the computer solution is well tested.
> (adapted from SCEMP, 1983).

It is also worth exploring alternatives to each organization acquiring its own computer system and training its own staff to use it. For instance, shared use of a more elaborate and expensive system may be preferable to buying a free-standing one; buying time on a large institutional computer may also be useful for certain kinds of tasks. Where an organization entirely lacks experience of computers but is nevertheless interested in the possibilities of computerization, it may be useful to try leasing or borrowing a computer system for experimental purposes before launching into a major scheme for computerization.

It may also be possible to draw professional help in programming and using the equipment from institutions who specialize in such advice (see Appendix 2) or from the new MSC-sponsored Information Technology Centres, which are supposed to be available for community use. Community organizations may also find that voluntary help of a limited kind is available from the many enthusiastic amateur and professional computer programmers: over its first two years SCEMP acquired considerable numbers of programs from such voluntary sources. Finally, organizations such as SCEMP in Scotland and the Community Computing Network in England may be able to offer general advice and information.

The Computer as Chameleon

The current enthusiasm for using computers in many organizations in community education has created a growing number of innovative and at least potentially helpful ways of using computers to support adult learning. The problems involved should by now be evident. They range from the often incomprehensible manuals that come with new computers to the dangers that important human relationships may be endangered by thoughtless or insensitive use of the machines. Again and again the fact emerges that computers are not useful for general purposes but rather to help to meet specific needs in specific ways.

Perhaps, in the end, computers in community education are more like Woody Allen's Zelig then like either Proteus or the Golem: their chameleon-like nature changes depending on their context and purposes. For those organizations in community education who make use of them, they can provide, if chosen and used appropriately, a valuable service which may help community education to reach more people more effectively. They can also be an important step in overcoming some of the tendency, created by other computer applications, towards an ever more divided society. The power and the versatility of computers could thus be harnessed to the good of the community as a whole rather than merely to benefit individuals and institutions who can afford them.

6

Computers for All?

> There is a world of difference between what computers can do and what society will choose to do with them.
>
> (Seymour Papert, 1980)

The power and the versatility of computers gives them an enormous potential to deform and to enhance our lives. As Papert sees, however, the determining factor in their ultimate impact is not what the machines can do in themselves but rather the human contexts in which they are introduced and the purposes for which they are used. In particular, as we have seen in Chapters 1 and 2, the social, economic and educational contexts into which computers are currently being introduced may exacerbate prevailing injustices.

If these graver consequences can be mitigated there are many ways in which computers can dramatically enhance adult learning. Chapter 3 has considered how educational computer programs might contribute directly to adult learning. Chapter 4 has shown how learning about computers is an important form of adult education. Chapter 5 has suggested how computers can support community education. For the future, there are many other possibilities for using computers in adult learning, which will be discussed later in this chapter.

There remain, of course, many limitations in using computers for adult learning, as Chapters 3 and 5 have tried to suggest. Chapters 4 and 5 argued that the effects of some of these difficulties can be alleviated by widespread education in computer literacy. In particular, adult and community educators who are fully aware of the limitations and possibilities of computers will be able to decide when computerization, despite its drawbacks, is appropriate — and when it is not.

But perhaps the most important of all the interconnections between computers and adult learning is the way in which computerization can contribute to a new understanding of the central role of adult and continuing education in society. Moreover, the main characteristics and effects of computers, which were discussed in Chapters 1 and 2, lend support to important new ways of thinking about adult learning. Specifically, computers may strengthen the argument for a pluralistic view of adult learning supported by networks of diverse experts.

This chapter is primarily concerned with these broader implications of computers and adult learning. It will look first at the potential for social, economic and educational divisiveness that is implied by the contexts and purposes of contemporary computers. These undesired effects of computerization will then be contrasted with the possibility that computers, especially through developments in artificial intelligence, may be able to emancipate adult learning and bring adults closer to one another, rather than exacerbate the divisions between them. There remain, however, far more unanswered questions than positive achievements in this area, and the chapter tries to acknowledge these difficulties. The last part of the chapter then hazards a guess at how computers may interact with adult learning to evolve new and constructive ways of thinking about both.

The Injustice of Computers

The use of word processors provides a striking illustration of how two different contexts for the same computerized process can have diametrically opposite effects:

> Because they eliminate retyping and simplify the process of changing the text, word processors are potentially liberating for people doing work for themselves: they save time and effort. But time-saving is not necessarily liberating for people who are *employed* to operate word processors. Under the circumstances, the only freedom the machine gives to the operator is the freedom to go on the next job. (Arnold, *et al.* 1982).

Similarly, the man who chooses to work on his computer at home, freed from the need to travel to work and from extraneous distractions, may experience a liberation that may not be so apparent to a colleague forced to work at home on her computer because she needs to care for dependents who compete for time and space with her work. The new 'cottage industry' of working at home by computer may increase personal liberation for some people while increasing the disadvantages for others. In particular, the fear has been expressed that with computerization 'a new group of exploited women workers will emerge as women forced out of the labour market by redundancy, lack of daycare and transportation turn to homeworking as a last resort' (Yanz and McCoy, 1983).

In general, where they are introduced primarily for economic gain, computers tend to aggravate existing disparities in social, economic, and educational matters. James Martin (1978), an enthusiastic proponent of the computerized society, depicts the 'advantages' of such developments:

> while part of humanity will be freed to enjoy more leisure, part will work 60 or 70 hour weeks. Some will be running worldwide activities via telecommunications; some will be creating the television needed to fill the numerous channels. Others will spend their time sitting in front of their wall screens with a carton of beer.

The clear implication here is that, with increasing computerization, the least adaptable and the least educated will become more so, while the most adaptable and the most highly educated pursue increasingly rewarding work.

The implication is not necessarily that those who do not work with computers will not work at all. At least in North America, there are predictions that certain jobs in service industries will increase more rapidly than employment in high technologies: the United States Bureau of Labor, for instance, projected in 1983 that in the next decade, three times as many janitors will be required as new computer systems analysts (Matas, 1983); in Canada, 'the less glamorous skills in the hospitality and fast-food industries are in greater demand than highly skilled computer programmers and technicians' (ibid).

One effect of computerization in our present economic climate may therefore be an increasing divide between those who work with their hands and those who work with computers. As Chapter 2 has already suggested, it appears that the forms of employment most likely to be adversely affected by computerization are the skilled and semi-skilled jobs that lie in between — particularly the kind of work in handling information that goes on in offices. In other words, computers may open up important gaps in our current social spectrum of occupations that stretch from unskilled to professional work.

Even if we leave aside the question of possible overall increases in unemployment, computers may exacerbate existing differences among various economic groups. There is an overall tendency of computerization to increase the strength of the strong and weaken the fragile, as many commentators have noted (see, for example, Laver, 1980; Sieghart, 1982; and Norman, 1981). At the same time, there is a probability of long-term unemployment in many Western countries, opening up the possibility of an even more extensive division between those who are employed and those who are not. Where they are introduced within these prevailing economic contexts, computers may aggravate rather than alleviate underlying injustices.

More specifically, the existence of a computer culture that is predominantly male will, unless checked, serve to increase further the sexual divisions within our society. Earlier chapters have already presented a smattering of the overwhelming evidence for the male bias of the world of computers. The phenomena, however, often goes unregarded: at 'Computers for All' exhibitions in Scotland, only female observers noticed the very substantial differences in numbers of males and females using the computers; male observers did not report any such bias. At present, there are few indications that such a bias will automatically correct itself with time; as the Equal Opportunities Commission has noted, computer studies are already assumed by many schools to be boys' subjects, along with nearly all the other sciences (Rogers, 1983).

It may also be that differences between men's and women's lives will continue to keep computers as a largely male preserve. Far more men than women are computer hobbyists, for reasons one can only speculate about: it might be that men have more time than women to pursue seriously hobbies that demand total concentration; it might be that men are particularly attracted to the kind of personal power promised by computers.

At home, too, few current developments in computer technology are likely to improve conditions of housework, which still dominates more women's than men's lives. Domestic robots are still a long way off; as Boden (1977) drily observes, 'it does not follow that the robot would be of much use in any house untidy enough to need it'. Even Martin's (1978) enthusiasm for reaching the wired society as soon as possible acknowledges that

> it will be a long time before the electronics industry produces robots for the home . . . even simple robots which can clear the table and keep the house clean. Instead, something immensely more interesting and valuable can emerge — communications products which . . . will fundamentally change work and travel patterns and vastly increase human capability.

Computers are unlikely to ease much of the domestic burdens of women, although they will offer enormous increases in potential to those people who are free to use them.

Educationally, we may wonder how far the benefits of computers will extend to everyone. Present training in computers, for instance, greatly favours males. In the developed world as a whole, women account for only 10 to 25 per cent of participants in higher skill-level computer courses (ILO, 1981). Comparable figures are not available for Britain as this book goes to press (because of computer breakdown at the MSC). Figures for Scotland, however, show that there is a striking difference between numbers of men and of women who completed TOPS courses in higher level computer skills in 1982: 70 men completed courses in programming and computer operating, as compared with 14 women (MSC, 1983).

In other forms of education, one might expect that computers will increase rather then diminish divisions among people. Certainly, computers remain a relatively expensive form of learning, and will thus be found more often where there are significant amounts of money to spend on education.

Nevertheless, learning with computers does offer ways of bridging the gap between those who are well-educated and those with little formal education. As we have discussed in Chapter 3, 4 and 5, computers as a medium for learning appear to be attractive to people with widely varying educational qualifications. In schools they are already used with students of greatly varying ability, ranging from sixth-form pupils sitting examinations in physics and mathematics to remedial pupils who have difficulty performing simple tasks in reading, spelling and calculating. So also in adult education, computers are used with a wide spectrum of learners, ranging from those entering adult basic education to university students who test complicated hypotheses on complex models and simulations.

It may be that as a learning tool computers already represent one important way in which many different kinds of adults may all be offered new learning experiences. The serious limitations in current learning by computers mean that these goals will not be reached merely by using computers, but as we shall see, careful, sensitive use of computers can help adult education to reach out to more kinds of learners than conventional provision can hope to do.

But broadly, we need to ask what adult education could hope to gain from any alliance with computers. In trying to answer this question, I shall look first at what appear to be some of the more promising paths currently being cleared in the jungle of computer developments. I shall then consider some obstacles that seem to lie in the way of using computers to enhance adult learning and shall suggest ways in which adult educators could start to dismantle these barriers.

New Learning Styles

Over the past few years, the sheer attractiveness of computers as both a subject and a method of learning has contributed to new patterns and new styles of learning. Perhaps the most important direction here has been the growth and development of family learning, both literally within people's homes and by analogy in more formal educational environments.

By 'family learning' I mean learning where different members of a close group contribute their different expertise to new situations. Where computers are involved, children tend to have at least as much to give to this kind of learning as adults, and both parents and children will therefore be likely to take part in such learning on more or less equal terms. The existence of such a family learning style based on computers is confirmed by so many recent computer advertisements that one can only suppose that it represents at least what people would like to happen, if not something that actually does take place in some homes.

In many cases, such learning is often merely at the level of learning how to use a new home computer ('Your kids will teach you how to use it', says a recent IBM advertisement for a personal computer) rather than for more systematic or academic learning. Regardless of the precise purposes for which it is used, such family learning does turn upside down the conventional assumption that parents teach children how to cope with their world.

There is also some limited evidence that family learning of this kind may be changing in a subtle way the composition of conventional classes in adult education. I personally know of a number of evening classes in computing, of the kind normally attended only by adults, which have recently admitted both children and their parents because of popular pressure to do so. Summer schools in computing too have expanded enormously in Britain over the past few years, and many of these offer parents and children the chance to study computers together.

Even where it has not taken such a literal form in adult education classes, the

MY SON EXPLAINED IT TO ME ON FRIDAY. I BOUGHT IT ON SATURDAY. AND AS OF MONDAY IT'S BEEN BEAVERING AWAY IN MY LITTLE SHOP.

Advertisement for IBM Personal Computer.

idea of family learning has metaphorically affected the way in which adults learn formally about computers. Demand in Britain for courses in computing has been so great over the past few years that it was impossible to meet merely by adult educators who were also qualified computer experts. As a result, in a number of instances adult tutors have undertaken classes on the agreed understanding with their students that both tutor and student would try to master the work together (Salkeld, 1983). Similarly, the members of the many computer clubs through the country willingly exchange their varied forms of expertise with one another.

Conventional hierarchies of tutor and student have little place in such 'families'. Indeed, as Papert (1980) notes, 'a very important feature of work with computers is that the teacher and the learner can be engaged in a real intellectual collaboration. . . . New situations that neither teacher nor learner has seen before come up frequently.' Learning about computers is therefore likely to be particularly congenial to those adults who choose to learn in what Hoggart (1983) calls 'communities' of learners.

New Learning Media

While it seems unlikely that the basic format of computers will change substantially over the next decade or so, there will probably be a number of ways in which computers will be increasingly linked with other media to offer more varied and sophisticated learning experiences than now exist. The amount of personal computing power that will be available to individuals who can afford it will increase considerably. This increase will expand and deepen the kinds of searching for information that can be carried out by a personal computer. The expansion of computer communication networks will make it more and more possible to search ever more widely for information, while the development of computer linked video equipment will enable deeper exploration of selected areas of enquiry.

One example of an important new learning medium that will enable students to search for information and knowledge in greater depth is the use of video disk equipment connected with a computer. Such a system, known as an 'interactive video disk', can allow students to call up separately any one of the 54,000 frames of information held on the disk, including still or moving pictures, text, diagrams and sound tracks.

The training possibilities of such a system are already considerable and are being steadily expanded. For instance, the Massachusetts Institute of Technology has developed a bicycle repair manual which uses interactive video combined with a television screen which is sensitive to touch. 'If the user touches any part of the bicycle shown on the screen, a moving picture shows exactly how that part works, in slow motion or speeded up. The user can zoom in or ask for more information on any part' (Hawkridge, 1983a).

The same principle — of enabling trainees to see how machines or other systems work without actually dismantling them — could, of course, be widely applied in training at many different levels. Indeed, it is already being used to train pilots of light planes, doctors and retail store managers (ibid). Within Britain, both the Open University and the National Extension College (among others) are experimenting with the training possibilities offered by such interactive video disks.

While interactive video disks will enable trainees and other learners to search for certain kinds of information and illustrations in depth, the linking of personal or institutional computers or terminals with one another by telephone lines increasingly allows learners to survey very large bodies of information. More and more libraries in particular are using terminals connected to a central computer to enable them to search millions of titles for information about specific topics. Individuals who have Prestel at home or who use it in public locations also have a way of getting up-to-date information about many different topics, although, as Chapter 5 noted, the educational value of the information so far available has not yet been established.

More and more such centralized computer information services are becoming available. So far they rarely seem to be used for predominantly educational purposes. Recent studies of the major uses of such services in American homes emphasize their advantages for managing financial matters (Hawkridge, 1983a), but they seem rarely to be used for learning. In Britain, too, 'Prestel for People' found that most people wanted information from Prestel about matters of general interest rather than educative 'social' information (Kania, 1983).

Even where such information services are not being used directly for learning, the fact that they are being used for information by both adults and children has important implications for adult education. Most adults today are not familiar with the skills required to make effective use of these kinds of centralized computer information services, and instructions for using them, as provided by the distributors, may often be inadequate. This gap between the information available and the skills needed to get hold of the information that is wanted clearly needs to be bridged.

There are also, as we shall see later, other broader educational implications of the increasing use of computerized information. But before we can consider these, we need first to sample some current developments in what may at first seem to be a field remote from adult learning but which has important implications for it — artificial intelligence.

Artificial Intelligence and Adult Learning

The field of artificial intelligence has recently received a great deal of attention primarily because of the potential commercial threat posed to many countries by Japan's 'Fifth Generation Computer Project', in which artificial intelligence is crucial. The overall idea of the Japanese project is to enable computers of the 1990s to understand Japanese and other natural languages, to interpret the speech of many different people, to act as intelligent assistants in many different tasks and to control advanced domestic and industrial robots (Boden, 1983).

That description of the aims of the project gives a general indication of what is included in the field of artificial intelligence. More specifically, artificial intelligence may be defined as 'the use of computer programs and programming techniques to cast light on the principles of intelligence in general and human thought in particular' (Boden, 1977). Human learning is thus one important facet of artificial intelligence.

The implications of this field of enquiry for adult learning are manifold, and include new ways of thinking about learning, the creation of computer programs that can help people to make decisions based on expert advice, and innovative methods of combining different kinds of professional expertise. We can sample some of these possibilities by looking first at one computer that helps doctors to make important decisions, and then at some of the contributions that research in artificial intelligence has made to models of learning and working together.

One of the major achievements of artificial intelligence so far has been the creation of 'expert systems', programs which can produce knowledge that is more accurate and more comprehensive than any one individual possesses. The best known example is a program called MYCIN, which advises doctors on the choice of antibiotics in treating infectious diseases.

Doctors can ask MYCIN for advice on identifying micro-organisms and treating them with appropriate antibiotic drugs. Most importantly, they can also ask for explanations of the advice provided, so that the doctor consulting the programs is free to use his or her own clinical judgement about the relative value of the advice offered by the program (Boden, 1977). Where errors or gaps are identified in the knowledge contained in the program, non-computer experts in microbiology can easily alter it (Turney and Jones, 1983). Analogous systems are currently used by and being developed for such fields as genetic engineering, chemical analysis and geological prospecting (Boden, 1983).

The increasing use of such 'expert systems' may have profound implications for the value that adults place on knowledge and may therefore diminish the regard in which certain kinds of factual learning are held. At the same time, the effective use of an 'expert system' requires a high degree of reasoning ability, of being able to make important connections and to appreciate why certain decisions are advisable.

Indeed, the use of programs in artificial intelligence may often require analytical skills of a high order. Programs already exist in which it is sometimes difficult to determine whether one is communicating with a computer or another human being, as may be seen in the following exchange between a person and ELIZA, a computer program designed to simulate a non-directive therapist (ELIZA's contributions appear in capitals):

> Men are all alike.
> IN WHAT WAY
> They're always bugging us about something or other.
> CAN YOU THINK OF A SPECIFIC EXAMPLE
> Well, my boyfriend made me come here.
> YOUR BOYFRIEND MADE YOU COME HERE
> He says I'm depressed much of the time.
> I AM SORRY TO HEAR THAT YOU ARE DEPRESSED
> It's true. I am unhappy.
> DO YOU THINK COMING HERE WILL HELP YOU NOT TO BE UNHAPPY
> I need some help, that much seems certain.
> WHAT WOULD IT MEAN TO YOU IF YOU GOT SOME HELP
> Perhaps I could learn to get along with my mother.
> TELL ME MORE ABOUT YOUR FAMILY
> My mother takes care of me.
> WHO ELSE IN YOUR FAMILY TAKES CARE OF YOU
> My father.
> YOUR FATHER
> You are like my father in some ways.
> WHAT RESEMBLANCE DO YOU SEE
> You are not very aggressive but I think you don't want me to notice that.
> WHAT MAKES YOU THINK I AM NOT VERY AGGRESSIVE
> You don't argue with me.
> DOES IT PLEASE YOU TO THINK I AM AFRAID OF YOU
> My father is afraid of everybody.
> WHAT ELSE COMES TO MIND WHEN YOU THINK OF YOUR FATHER
> Bullies.
> DOES THAT HAVE ANYTHING TO DO WITH THE FACT THAT YOUR BOYFRIEND MADE YOU COME HERE (Weizenbaum, 1966)

It may be that using programs in artificial intelligence does not merely encourage us to develop skills of a high analytical kind. Programs such as ELIZA may also raise important issues about the role that human beings play in communicating and learning with one another. These are all matters with which adult educators are intimately concerned and which they can sometimes explore further through work in artificial intelligence.

The second major area in which artificial intelligence seems to have implications for adult learning concerns how workers in artificial intelligence think about thinking. There are a number of ways in which 'the computational way of thinking about thinking' (Boden, 1977) may be helpful to ways of thinking about adult learning.

In the first place, the way in which programs are written in artificial intelligence — and, indeed, in all forms of computer work — provides a positive way of responding to errors or mistakes. For computer programmers the failure of a program to do what they want it to is not a threatening experience but one which can be remedied by discovering what is wrong with the program and altering it accordingly. This process, which is known somewhat inelegantly but usefully as 'debugging', is often a complicated one and is, of course, not always successful. But the attitudes to failure that it encourages may be a helpful model of learning, particularly for those adults who perceive their previous attempts at learning as failures.

More generally, work that is currently taking place in both America and Britain with children using the programming language LOGO, developed by research in artificial intelligence, suggests that there may be a number of ways in which computers can liberate people from previously constrained thinking. Papert (1980) claims, for instance, that 'contact with the computer can open access to knowledge for people, not instrumentally by providing them with processed information, but by challenging constraining assumptions they make about themselves'.

With many others who work in artificial intelligence, Papert argues that computers 'can help people form new relationships with knowledge that cut across the traditional lines separating humanities from sciences and knowledge of the self from both of these'. How far these claims can be substantiated in practice is still a matter for debate. There are, however, fascinating possibilities of using computers in an analogous way to help adults learn *how* to learn.

Finally, the very nature of work within the field of artificial intelligence has interesting implications for those educators who believe in interdisciplinary approaches to adult learning. Researchers in artificial intelligence include a wide range of experts who collaborate on problems of common interest: they include computer scientists, physicists, engineers and applied mathematicians together with philosophers, psychologists and educators. The way in which they share expertise and communicate with one another may well be one model for the kinds of contact that now need to take place between adult educators and computer specialists.

Limitations to Development

I am not attempting to sketch scenarios for the ways in which computers, and associated work in artificial intelligence, may affect adult learning in the future. Rather, I have glanced at some current developments which seem to be relevant to adult learning, in order to suggest that people working in adult education could have more in common than they might have realized with workers in artificial intelligence. There are, however, a number of important constraints which may inhibit the development of these and many other possibilities, and any speculation about what could happen will have to take account of them.

In the first place, we cannot assume that things that are theoretically possible will necessarily ever take place. Within artificial intelligence, there are phenomena whose complexity makes it highly unlikely that adequate simulation

> will ever in fact be achieved. This applies to 'common-sense' knowledge and linguistic ability of the type attributed to the fictional HAL, not only to triumphs of the human imagination like superlative literary and scientific creativity. (Boden, 1977).

The development of sophisticated computer tutors, for instance, is dependent on our knowing more than we currently do about 'the way in which human students build, and progressively modify, internal representations of concepts and skills' (ibid).

As well as these theoretical problems, there remain many practical barriers to using computers extensively in adult learning. The cost of the equipment itself is rapidly falling, but it remains relatively expensive, at least for the many under-financed providers of adult education. The cost of developing programs for the equipment is an even more serious constraint: 'computer-aided instruction. . . . to be used effectively, require[s] long and complex programme production' (Sharples, 1982a), and such preparation is costly.

To give a rough idea of the probable cost, the lowest estimated time required to produce sixty minutes of an educational program is about one hundred hours (Canada Science Council, 1982). At the Open University, 'experience from science course teams shows that to produce thirty minutes of interesting activity for students at a terminal takes several persons months of activity. Our experience of the minimum effort required to produce this half hour is one month of an academic's time and one month from a member of the Academic Computing Service' (Scanlon *et al.*, 1982). The BBC estimate for producing substantial programs ranges from £5,000 to £10,000 (Radcliffe and Salkeld, 1983).

In addition to the sheer cost of professional programming, there is the further difficulty that — as we have noted earlier — there are as yet few people who combine training, experience and skill in adult education with knowledge of computers. The Scottish Community Education Microelectronics Project noted in its first year that 'there seems generally in Scotland . . to be a relative lack of educators who are familiar with both community and computer education' (SCEMP, 1982b). The position does not appear to be very different in the rest of the world.

Brakes on development also stem from the highly fragmented and very diverse nature of adult learning. Commercial development of computerized learning depends on large, relatively homogeneous markets for programs, but adult education is unlikely to provide such a market. Nor, as we have seen in Chapter 5, is community education likely to be homogeneous in its needs.

Additional constraints arise from the ever-present technical problems with computer equipment in use: as the team working on the implementation of the Open University CYCLOPS System typically found, 'a great deal of our time was spent solving technical faults in the equipment, much of which had not been anticipated' (McConnell, 1982). As Hawkridge (1983a) observes, 'we are not being offered immaculate technology, infinitely reliable, adaptable and flexible'.

There may also be considerable resistance by some adult students to the prospect of using a computer at all. Experience at the Open University suggests that new users often find computer terminals difficult to use, may be embarrassed at using them with others in the room, and may be afraid of secret assessment by the computer (Scanlon *et al.*, 1982). And, as Chapter 5 showed, the older the student the less willing he or she may be to use the computer. Moreover, as they are currently presented, computers seem to be more attractive to male than to female users; any extensive use of computers for adult learning could thus place women at a particular disadvantage.

These constraints, however, are by no means all inherent in computers themselves. Even where the problems do arise from the very nature of computing, there are often ways of resolving them. As we have seen in Chapter 5, technical problems are not in themselves a barrier to using computers, provided that adequate account is taken of them in planning learning experiences. After all, human tutors sometimes fall ill, and strikes occasionally make it difficult to use particular buildings exactly as planned.

The problem that some adults dislike using computers can often be resolved by creating programs that welcome and encourage new users, as the Scottish Community Education Microelectronics Project has shown. Taking particular care not to allow young people, with their often intimidating computer skills, to dominate computer sessions is also an effective way of encouraging adults. The BBC Computer Literacy Project, notable for the way in which it attracted adults who had been anxious about computers, deliberately eschewed showing 'examples of impressively competent youngsters, which would be likely to increase the anxieties of older viewers' (Radcliffe and Salkeld, 1983).

Similarly, the problem of male dominance of computers is not inherent in computers themselves. It is perfectly possible, as the BBC's first two television series on computer literacy have shown, to attract almost equal numbers of women and men to computers. The significant factor here appears to be the deliberate choice of material which will appeal to women as well as to men and the inclusion of both women and men to present and illustrate the material (ibid).

Much the same considerations apply to making older people and lower socio-economic groups feel at home with computers; again, the BBC has shown how effectively adult computer education can appeal to all sectors of society by careful attention to their needs and preferences. In any case, it is already accepted throughout adult education that different learners have different preferences for methods of learning. Seen in this context of the need to provide a variety of ways into learning, computers can form one attractive path for at least some adults.

The problem that only a limited number of adult learners might use any one computer program is more deep-rooted, and there is no straightforward way of resolving it. Certainly, any commercially available programs for adult learning will be either few, expensive or both. Nevertheless, there are already publicly available programs in certain areas of adult learning — in health and in various other forms of community education, as we saw in Chapters 3 and 5. It is also possible that more of those public agencies who produce programs for children's learning may be persuaded to take account of adult learning. The programs which are available through the BBC's Telesoftware service, for instance, are free, but their main intended audience is children.

Adult educators who are interested in the possibilities of developing programs for adult learning might also consider the example of the Scottish Community Education Microelectronics Project, which has shown what may be achieved in producing programs for adults even on a small budget. SCEMP acquired over twenty programs mainly by drawing on the voluntary help of individuals and institutions who were so interested in the possibilities of computing that they willingly contributed their expertise. There are obvious limitations to the kinds of programs that can be produced by such networks. Nevertheless, it is worth noting that many educational institutions, computer clubs and the MSC's Information Technology Centres are all possible sources of computer programs for adult educators who approach them with specific ideas.

Perhaps, however, the problem needs to be re-stated. While it is unlikely that there will ever be a sufficient market for adult learning programs to justify widespread commercial provision, there may be certain areas of high demand where publicly provided programs are justifiable, as with programs to provide information and advice about careers, educational opportunities or welfare benefits, as we saw in Chapter 5. In other areas, programs that allow for local variation of centrally provided structures or information may be feasible at justifiable cost: as we saw in Chapter 3, for instance, some of the SCEMP programs allow local organizations or individuals to create their own variants within an overall uniform structure.

Overall, the tasks of engaging computers in adult learning reach well beyond the mere use of computer programs, as this book has tried to suggest throughout. In all of the areas concerned — programs for education and training, computer literacy, programs for community use — adult educators will increasingly find it necessary to draw on help from outside their own expertise. The BBC team for the Computer Literacy Project was able to achieve its notable successes because

> the project team had spent a great deal of time and effort maintaining close links with a whole range of outside organizations, the Departments of Education and Science, and Industry, the Microelectronics Education Programme, the Scottish Microelectronics Development Programme, the Council for Educational Technology, the National Extension College, local education authorities, and many others. (Radcliffe and Salkeld, 1983).

On a much smaller scale, the same pattern of networking seems to have been responsible for the successes of the Scottish Community Education Microelectronics Project. It too has drawn on a wide variety of sources of expertise and practical help, including universities, colleges, schools, Health Boards, the Scottish Health Education Group, the Scottish Council for Educational Technology, the Scottish Microelectronics Development Programme, voluntary organizations and various branches of central and local government.

At the crudest possible level, in its first year SCEMP estimated that such help multiplied its budget from £16,000 to approximately £70,000 (SCEMP, 1982b). More importantly, it demonstrated the real benefits of networking to produce such positive achievements as mounting public computer exhibitions, creating computer programs for adults, encouraging the use of computers in voluntary organizations and training community education staff in the use of computers.

In some ways, however, all of these developments in computers and adult learning represent only the tip of a massive iceberg. The major problem that computers now present for adult education is enabling people to make use of them for their own purposes and to reach their own decisions about them. Even if adult educators feel unduly restricted by the sheer practical limitations of using computers for learning, they will have to take account of a world that is being increasingly dominated by computerization.

The forces behind these developments are so powerful and so locked into the whole structure of our society that any attempt to ignore them is merely to yield them still greater power. As Chapters 2 and 4 argued, adult education has a major obligation to meet the need for computer literacy as well as responding to the other ways in which computers are changing all our lives: 'no adult can claim to be educated who does not have some knowledge of the sciences and technology as they increasingly affect all our lives' (ACACE, 1981).

Adult Learning and Computers: the Challenge

Whether it makes use of computers for its own purposes or not, adult learning will increasingly be affected by them in a number of ways. In the first place, adult educators may find that because computers are available to perform certain tasks, there is an even greater emphasis on those things that people do supremely well. Where computers can provide significant amounts of information and even knowledge, the adult educator will increasingly become the kind of person described by Legge (1982) — someone who facilitates learning, who helps people diagnose and clarify their requirements, advises them about the choice of educational methods and activities, encourages them through difficult periods and stimulates them to go forward.

Meanwhile, as the availability of computers gradually reinforces this role of adult educators, the impact of computerization on employment will mean that educating and training for changing occupations will become increasingly important. Already, the working lives of men and women are becoming more

"What it comes down to is this thing is capable of telling us a lot more than we really want to know.'

fluid and diverse, with fewer people remaining tied to a single occupation throughout their lives. Consequently, there will be a need for the kind of flexibility and adaptability that result from a broad general education and understanding of society.

With these needs, adult education will have to assume a more central role in public policy-making than it has done hitherto. The effects of computerization thus underline and reinforce the conclusions of the Alexander Report which said that 'the education of adults must be accepted as an essential component of national policy. The view of adult education as a marginal enterprise serving the interests of a relatively small proportion of the population can no longer be justified' (SED, 1975).

Here the traditional pattern of many women's lives may provide a helpful analogy by which to think about this changing nature of adult education. As Hughes and Kennedy (1985) argue, the fragmentation in most women's lives may actually be a positive and creative model for adult education, since it flexibly fits people's changing lifestyles and our current technological revolution. Hughes and Kennedy suggest that women fulfil a multiplicity of roles which are not seen in isolation from one another, whereas men's life patterns tend to run in parallel and rarely come together. For many men, work is separated from home and home is separated from most leisure activities. But for most women, the various roles that they fill tend to be criss-crossed and overlapping, with hierarchies more difficult to establish.

Interestingly enough, this interdependency amongst women's multiple roles may have an analogy in one important feature of computer programming as it is explored in artificial intelligence. The various parts of many computer programs inter-relate in complex ways with one another, often to form a heterarchical rather than a purely hierarchical pattern (Boden, 1977).

This apparent similarity between the dominant form of women's experience and the structure of many computer programs may suggest that there are valuable ways in which adult educators can respond to both. In particular, the analogy implies that adult education needs to find many specific ways in which to support the very diverse needs of adults. The BBC discovered at an early stage that there was more than one potential audience for computer literacy. The 'wide variations in expertise, expectation and need, on the part of potential viewers' necessitated a 'multi-layered learning system through which viewers could follow up their interest in computing to whatever level they wished' (Radcliffe and Salkeld, 1983).

Such a pluralistic approach to computer literacy was also advocated by Banks (1983) in his study of evening classes for adults, while Hughes and Kennedy support the need for adult education to make more specific provisions to meet the very different needs of women at the various stages of the major changes in their lives. It may be that the pluralistic model, derived from computer literacy, is more widely applicable as a way of responding to the changes in roles and way of living that computers have now created for all of us.

What remains certain is that the enormous flexibility that many women's lives already demand of them will have to become a pattern for all of us. It may also be that the way women organize their lives can give us an important model for responding to the social changes that will confront us as the result of increasing computerization.

The full implication of computers is that there will simply be less work to be done by people to meet their everyday needs (see, for instance, Jones, 1982). How societies respond to this problem will tend to determine whether they move towards increasing cohesion or increasing divisiveness. Where the available work is shared amongst all of us and where both computers and people work at those things each does best, there is a good chance that computers will help everyone to a fuller life. Where society divides into those who work and those who do not, however, there is too much of a chance that those who currently have power, education and wealth will increasingly have more of everything while those who are now without will have even less in the future.

What role can adult education play in this future? I have already suggested that the 'spreading of adult computer literacy is an immediate and major task facing adult educators' (Bostock and Seifert, 1983a). Beyond this general contribution, adult educators, if they reach out to those people who are actually computerizing our society, can help ensure that the needs of ordinary adults are taken into account when planning computer applications.

The problem now is that:

> the computer industry doesn't understand how adults learn. . . . The problem arises from the fact that software producers and manual writers are computer engineers or have been trained by computer engineers. They understand how the machine works but have no idea about how adults learn. Consequently, their software and manuals are geared to teaching us how the machine works rather than helping us learn how to use the machine to perform the real-life tasks we buy it to perform for us. As a result, we users find the instructions we get from the manuals, the software and the manufacturers' representatives to be confusing, irrelevant and frustrating in learning to use the computer for *our* purposes. (Knowles, 1983).

Here people who are trained and skilled in educating adults could clearly help in designing computer experiences for adults. Indeed, adult educators must do so if adults are ever to have a chance to use computers to their own benefit with as much facility and ease as their children already use them. Adult educators therefore need to include men and women who are working in the computer industry among their potential clients.

In order for adult educators to serve in this area effectively, we need new ways of sharing expertise with people in other fields. As we have already seen earlier in this chapter, workers in artificial intelligence have found ways of combining the expertise of very diverse disciplines where they are directed at solving common problems. Similarly, adult educators could try working together with computer experts rather than trying to acquire complex computer skills themselves. As the BBC Computer Literacy Project and the Scottish Community Education Microelectronics Project have shown, one can create networks of diverse talents who can together enhance adult learning by computers.

When we look at the full implications of computerizing our world, they include the possibility that we shall in the end make ourselves extinct by a nuclear war; there may be, as Legge (1982) so graphically says, a 'race between education and catastrophe'. If we are not to disadvantage ourselves in this race, we must not despise or reject the power of the computers which make possible the war that may in the end destroy us.

The computer in some ways may be like Hephaestus who, as god of fire and crafts, was so ugly that he was thrown out of Olympus. He is *The God that Limps* as Norman (1981) has characterized contemporary technology, but he is not therefore a devil. The purposes for which the power and versatility of the computer are used are human choices; they are not the inevitable consequences of the machines themselves.

Therefore, adult learners and those who provide for them should not try to fling this ugly god out of their homes. Rather, we should find ways of insisting that he will serve our real needs. We want our children to believe that people are in charge of technologies rather than dominated by them. The process of being able to control them for our own purposes begins with our learning, as adults, how to master them.

Appendix 1: A Layman's Guide to the Language of Educational Computing

The terms below are often encountered in reading about the uses of computers in education. Larger computer vocabularies appear in the dictionaries referred to in Appendix 2.

Alphanumeric. Containing both letters of the alphabet and numbers, as in 'alphanumeric keyboard'.

Artificial intelligence. Computer programs which attempt to emulate the processes of human thinking.

Author language. A programming language designed to help non-programmers write educational computer programs.

BASIC. Currently the most widely used programming language for microcomputers; the initials stand for 'Beginner's All-purpose Symbolic Instruction Code'.

Bug. An error in a computer program.

Computer. An electronic machine that stores and manipulates data by following detailed instructions.

Computer assisted learning (CAL). One of the most widely accepted terms for using computers for educational purposes.

Computer assisted instruction (CAI). Using a computer for teaching purposes. In Britain the term often implies a highly pedagogical approach.

Computer based education (CBE). Another term for using computers for educational purposes.

Computer based learning (CBL). Another term for using computers for educational purposes.

Computer managed instruction (CMI). Using computers to help with the routine management tasks in teaching, such as assessing, suggesting courses of study and keeping records.

Computer managed learning (CML). Using computers to help with the routine management tasks in teaching and learning.

Courseware. Computer materials used for teaching and learning. Some computer programs are of this type, whereas others are used to make the computer operate.

Cursor. A mark that appears on the screen of a computer to show the user where the next character will appear once he or she enters it on the keyboard.

Data. Any numbers, words or other symbols that are manipulated by a computer.

Data base. A highly organized collection of data that can be searched to yield specific information.

Data processing. The manipulation of symbols by a computer.

Debug. The process of finding and correcting an error in a computer program.

Dedicated. A term for using a computer for one particular purpose rather than for a whole range of functions.

Disk. A thin magnetic device that holds a large amount of data for use by a computer. A floppy disk is generally used with a relatively small computer and holds much less data than a hard disk, which is generally used with a mainframe or a mini computer.

Disk drive. A machine which holds a disk and transmits the data on it to and from a computer very quickly.

Documentation. Notes about the content and purposes of a computer program.

Down. Term used of a computer that is not working.

Drill and practice. An instructional program in which the learner is given a highly structured sequence of exercises.

Frame. One step in an educational computer program; it might consist, for instance, of a few sentences presenting information or concepts, followed by a question, the learner's answer and, depending on the answer, a suggestion about which frame to go to next.

GIGO. Stands for 'garbage in, garbage out', referring to the fact that unreliable data inevitably produces unreliable results.

Graphics. The visual material (other than text) that appears on the screen of a computer; it can include drawings, lines, graphs, charts, maps, and moving images.

Hands-on. A popular term for practical experience of a computer.

Hardware. The various pieces of equipment used in computing.

Information. Meaningful data or symbols.

Information retrieval. The process of getting useful information by searching a large amount of data.

Information technology. An umbrella term which usually refers to the use of computers and telecommunications systems linked to them.

Interactive. Refers to the situation in which a user gives information to a computer which then gives a rapid response.

Mainframe computer. The largest kind of computer.

Memory. Where a computer finds its instructions and its data and stores its results.

Menu. A list of choices displayed on a computer.

Menu-driven. A computer program in which the user is required to choose from a list of options to enable the program to continue.

Microcomputer. The smallest kind of computer.

Minicomputer. A medium sized computer.

Model. An analogue of real-life situation or system which can be used to elicit information about the likely behaviour of the real situation or system.

Modem. A device which enables computers to communicate over telephone wires.

Monitor. A term frequently used to refer to the television-like screen by which many computers display information.

Network. A system in which computers communicate with one another.

On-line. When information is sent directly to a computer for immediate processing.

Peripheral. Any device which is attached to a computer but not essential for using it, such as a printer or a monitor.

Printer. Equipment that prints out information from the computer line by line.

Program. The instructions that tell a computer what to do.

Programming language. A symbolic code which allows a programmer to communicate with a computer; there are many different programming languages which bear variable relationships to English.

QWERTY. Refers to the keyboard layout of a standard typewriter which is used for most computer keyboards; the letters represent the first six letters of the keyboard.

Routing. The process of guiding learners through a course based on the assumption that most of them will follow a few well-used paths.

Simulation. An analogue of a real-life situation or system which can be used to elicit information about the real system.

Software. Computer programs.

Systems analyst. Someone who analyses how best to put computers to work in specific situations.

Telesoftware. Computer programs which are broadcast.

Teletext. Computer-based information which is broadcast and can be seen on television sets adapted to receive it.

Terminal. A device for communicating with a computer, usually consisting of a keyboard, a monitor and perhaps a printer.

Time-sharing. When more than one person uses the same computer at the same time.

Up-date. To change the information in a program so that it is up to date.

User friendly. Refers to a computer and/or programs which are supposed to be easy for beginners to use.

VDU. Stands for visual display unit; an alternative term for a monitor.

Videotext. The generic term for teletext and viewdata; refers to computer-generated information displayed at a distance by a television screen.

Viewdata. Refers to computer-generated information which is communicated over telephone wires and displayed on a television screen; in Britain the best known public system of this kind is Prestel.

Appendix 2: Sources of Information and Advice

Already there are substantial sources of information, discussion, and advice about the uses of computers in certain branches of formal education, particularly in schools and to a lesser extent in further and higher education. These areas have developed their own professional literature and networks, and readers who wish to pursue their enquiries at such a sophisticated level may simply skip to the last entries in the material cited below.

Others may prefer to explore further some of the issues raised in individual chapters of this book before tackling the more demanding literature, which is often addressed to fellow professionals in educational computing. The entries under the chapter headings below therefore refer primarily to works which are accessible to anyone who is interested, but not necessarily fluent, in the field of computers and adult learning.

1. 'Why Computers Matter'

ACACE, 1983. 'Microtechnology and the Education of Adults'. Leicester, Advisory Council for Adult and Continuing Education.

Evans, Christopher, 1980. *The Mighty Micro: The Impact of the Micro-Chip Revolution*. Sevenoaks, Hodder and Stoughton.

Hawkridge, David, 1983. *New Information Technology in Education*. London, Croom Helm.

2. 'The Character of Computers'

Bradbeer, Robin, De Bono, Peter and Laurie, Peter, 1982. *The Computer Book: An Introduction to Computers and Computing*. London, BBC Publications.

Burkitt, Alan, and Williams, Elaine, 1981. *The Silicon Civilisation*. London, W. H. Allen.

Computers and Computing 1982 —. Open University Course PM252.

Dertouzos, Michael, and Moses, Joel (eds.), 1979. *The Computer Age: A Twenty Year View*. Cambridge, Mass., MIT Press.

Forester, Tom (ed.), 1980. *The Microelectronics Revolution: The Complete Guide to the New Technology and its Impact on Society*. Oxford, Basil Blackwell.

Forster, E. M., 1947. 'The Machine Stops', in *The Collected Tales*. New York, Alfred Knopf.
Orwell, George, 1954. *Nineteen Eighty-four*. Harmondsworth, Penguin Books.
Prenis, John, 1981. *The Language of Computers*. London, W. H. Allen.

3. 'Learning with Computers'

BBC TV. *The Learning Machine* (projected television programme 1984).
Bostock, Stephen and Seifert, Roger, 1983. 'Introducing a Microcomputer into Adult Education Classes'. *Adult Education*, Vol. 55, No. 4.
Micros in Schools 1982 —. Open University Packs for Teachers.
Rushby, Nicholas, 1979. *An Introduction to Educational Computing* London, Croom Helm.
SCEMP, 1982. 'Computers for All: Report on Work in Progress'. Edinburgh, Scottish Council for Community Education.
SCEMP, 1982. 'Computers for All: Report on Work in Progress', 2nd edition. Glasgow, Scottish Community Education Microelectronics Project.
SCEMP, 1982. 'Guidelines for the Design of Computer Programs for Community Use'. Glasgow, Scottish Microelectronics Development Programme.

The following organizations, among others, offer information and advice in the field of learning with computers:
The Computer Referral Service, P.O. Box 7, London W3 6XJ.
Council for Educational Technology, 3 Devonshire Street, London.
Microelectronics Education Programme, Cheviot House, Coach Lane Campus, Newcastle-upon-Tyne.
Microelectronics Educational Development Centre, Paisley College, High Street, Paisley.
Scottish Community Education Microelectronics Project, Dowanhill, 74 Victoria Crescent Road, Glasgow.

4. 'Learning about Computers'

BBC TV. *The Computer Programme*, 1982 —. Available on video from BBC Enterprises Ltd, Educational and Training Sales, Woodlands, 80 Wood Lane, London W12 0TT.
BBC TV. *Making the Most of the Micro*, 1983 —. Available on video from BBC Enterprises Ltd, address above.
Radcliffe, John, and Salkeld, Roberts, 1983. *Towards Computer Literacy: The BBC Computer Literacy Project 1979–1983*. London, BBC Publications.

5. 'Computers and Community Education'

BBC TV. *The Electronic Office*, 1984.
Covvey, Dominic, and McAlister, Neil, 1982. *Computer Choices: Beware of Conspicuous Computing*. Reading, Mass., Addison-Wesley.

Ottley, Penny, and Kempson, Elaine, 1982. 'Computer Benefits?' London, National Consumer Council.

SCEMP, 1983. 'Report on Work in Progress', 3rd ed. Glasgow, Scottish Community Education Microelectronics Project.

The following organizations, among others, offer information and advice in the field of computers and community education:

Community Computing Network, c/o Pete Rowan, Old School House, Irish Street, Whitehaven, Cumbria.

Scottish Community Education Microelectronics Project, address above.

6. 'Computers for All?'

Boden, Margaret, 1977. *Artificial Intelligence and Natural Man*. Hassocks, Harvester Press.

Jones, Barry, 1982. *Sleepers, Wake! Technology and the Future of Work*. Brighton, Wheatsheaf Books.

Sieghart, Paul (ed.), 1982. *Micro-Chips with Everything: The Consequences of Information Technology*. London, Comedia Publishing Group in association with the Institute of Contemporary Arts.

Knowles, Malcolm, 1983. 'Malcolm Knowles Finds a Worm in his Apple'. *Training and Development Journal*, May.

Laver, Murray, 1980. *Computers and Social Change*. Cambridge, University Press.

Weizenbaum, Joseph, 1976. *Computer Power and Human Reason*. San Francisco, Freeman.

Ways into the Professional Literature

O'Shea, Tim, and Self, John, 1983. *Learning and Teaching with Computers*. Brighton, Harvester.

Papert, Seymour, 1980. *Mindstorms: Children, Computers and Powerful Ideas*. Brighton, Harvester.

Rushby, Nick (ed.), 1981. *Selected Readings in Computer-based Learning*. London, Kogan Page.

The papers published by members of the Open University Computer Assisted Learning Group at the Institute of Educational Technology are also helpful. Geoffrey Crowther Building, The Open University, Walton Hall, Milton Keynes, MK7 6AA.

Journals:

British Journal of Educational Technology
Computer Education
Educational Computing
Educational Technology
Phase Two

References

ACACE, 1981. Cited in Stephen Bostock and Roger Seifert, 'Computer Integration and Computer Literacy'.

ACACE, 1982a. *Adults: their Educational Experience and Needs*. Leicester, Advisory Council for Adult and Continuing Education.

ACACE, 1982b. *Continuing Education: From Policies to Practice*. Leicester, Advisory Council for Adult and Continuing Education.

ACACE, 1983. 'Microtechnology and the Education of Adults'. Leicester, Advisory Council for Adult and Continuing Education.

Adult Education: The Challenge of Change, 1975 (The Alexander Report), Edinburgh, Scottish Education Department.

Adult Education: A Plan for Development, 1973 (The Russell Report), London, Department of Education and Science.

ALBSU, [1982]. 'The Use of Microcomputers in Basic Education'. London, Adult Literacy and Basic Skills Unit.

Allason, Julian, 1983. 'Micros Smash the Million Mark'. *The Observer*, March 27.

Arnold, Erik, Burke, Lynda and Faulkner, Wendy, 1982. 'Women and Microelectronics: The Case of Word Processors', in Rothschild, Joan (ed.), *Women, Technology and Innovation*.

Banks, David, 1983. 'Adult Classes in Computing: A Survey'. *Adult Education*, Vol. 56, No. 1.

Barrett, Kristen, 1982. Personal communication at SCEMP.

BBC, 1981. 'The Computer Literacy Project'. London, unpublished BBC Broadcasting Research Special Report.

BBC, 1983. 'BBC's Computer Literacy Project: An Evaluation'. London, unpublished BBC Broadcasting Research Special Report.

Boden, Margaret, 1977. *Artificial Intelligence and Natural Man*. Hassocks, Harvester Press.

Boden, Margaret, 1983. 'A New Generation of Machines'. *The Times Higher Education Supplement*. June 17.

Bostock, Stephen, and Seifert, Roger, 1983a. 'Introducing a Microcomputer into Adult Education Classes'. *Adult Education*, Vol. 55, No. 4.

Bostock, Stephen, and Seifert, Roger, 1983b. 'Computer Integration and Computer Literacy', in ACACE, 'Micro technology and the Education of Adults'.

Bradbeer, Robin, De Bono, Peter, and Laurie, Peter, 1982. *The Computer Book: An Introduction to Computers and Computing*. London, BBC Publications.

Burkitt, Alan, and Williams, Elaine, 1980. *The Silicon Civilisation*. London, W. H. Allen.

Burton, Maggie, 1983. 'The Dream Machine'. *Personal Computer World*, July.

Butler, David, 1981. *Britain and the Information Society*. London, Haydon and Son.

Canada Science Council, 1982. Cited in Lina Trudel and Paul Belanger, 'Computerization: For Better and for Worse'.

CNAA, 1982. 'Implications of the Development of Information Technology for CNAA Undergraduate Courses'. London, Council for National Academic Awards.

Cooley, 1980. Cited in Arnold, Erik *et al.*, 'Women and Microelectronics; The Case of Word Processors'.

Covvey, Dominic, and McAlister, Neil, 1982. *Computer Choices: Beware of Conspicuous Computing*. Reading, Mass., Addison-Wesley.

Dean, Christopher, and Whitlock, Quintin, 1983. *A Handbook of Computer Based Training*. London, Kogan Page.

Deken, Joseph, 1981. *The Electronic Cottage*. New York, William Morrow.

Dertouzos, Michael, and Moses, Joel, (eds), 1979. *The Computer Age: A Twenty Year View*. Cambridge, Mass., MIT Press.

Eason, Ken, 1982. 'Human Factors in Information Technology'. *Physics in Technology*, September.

ECCTIS, 1983. 'Advance Notice'. Milton Keynes, Educational Counselling and Credit Transfer Information Service.

Eliot, T. S., 1958. 'Choruses from *The Rock*, in *Collected Poems*. London, Faber and Faber.

Evans, Christopher, 1980. *The Mighty Micro: The Impact of the Micro-Chip Revolution*. Sevenoaks, Hodder and Stoughton.

Forester, Tom (ed.), 1980. *The Microelectronics Revolution: The Complete Guide to the New Technology and its Impact on Society*. Oxford, Basil Blackwell.

Forster, E. M., 1947. 'The Machine Stops', in *The Collected Tales*. New York, Alfred Knopf.

Freeman, Richard, 1983. Personal communication at the National Extension College, Cambridge.

Frogbrook, Peter, 1983. 'Educational Counselling and Credit Transfer Information Service'. Milton Keynes, ECCTIS.

Gartside, Peter, 1982. 'Six Courses Linked to the BBC Computer Literacy Project'. Glasgow, Scottish Council for Educational Technology.

Gibbons, Sue, and Simpson, Ormond, 1982. 'Let the Computer Take the Strain'. *Teaching at a Distance*, Vol. 22.

Harris, Sidney, 1982. *What's so Funny about Computers*? Los Altos, Calif., William Kaufmann.

Hawkridge, David, 1983a. *New Information Technology in Education*. London, Croom Helm.

Hawkridge, David, 1983b. 'Teachers Put IT to Good Use'. *The Times Higher Education Supplement*, June 17.

Hoggart, Richard, 1983. 'ACACE 1977–1983: A Personal Statement by the Chairman', Leicester, Advisory Council for Adult and Continuing Education.

Home Office, 1983. 'An Evaluation of the Use of PLATO in Aylesbury Prison'. London, unpublished internal report.

Hooper, Richard, 1977. *The National Development Programme in Computer Assisted*

Learning: Final Report of the Director. London, Council for Educational Technology.

Howe, Jim, n.d. 'Artificial Intelligence and Computer Assisted Instruction: Ten Years on'. Edinburgh, Department of Artificial Intelligence, University of Edinburgh.

Hughes, Mary, and Kennedy, Mary, 1985. *New Futures: Women, Education and Change*. London, Routledge and Kegan Paul. To be published.

ILO, 1981. Cited in Diane Werneke, *Microelectronics and Office Jobs: The Impact of the Chip on Women's Employment*.

Jones, Barry, 1982. *Sleepers, Wake! Technology and the Future of Work*. Brighton, Wheatsheaf Books.

Jones, Ann, and Scanlon, Eileen (eds), 1981. 'A review of Research in the CAL Group: A Report of the First Annual Conference, November'. Milton Keynes, Open University (CAL Research Group Technical Report No. 27).

Kania, Helena, 1983. 'Prestel for People . . .' London, Council for Educational Technology.

Kidd, Roby, 1973. Cited in Robert Smith, *Learning How to Learn: Applied Theory for Adults*.

Knowles, Malcolm, 1983. 'Malcolm Knowles Finds a Worm in his Apple'. *Training and Development Journal*, May.

Lamb, John, 1983. '£44M Allocated to Making UK Computers "Friendlier" '. *The Scotsman*, October 10.

Laver, Murray, 1980. *Computers and Social Change*. Cambridge, Cambridge University Press.

Lean, Elizabeth, 1983. 'Byting Back: The Industry Responds'. *Training and Development Journal*, May.

Legge, Derek, 1981. 'Development of Information, Guidance and Counselling Services'. Amersfoort, European Bureau of Adult Education.

Legge, Derek, 1982. *The Education of Adults in Britain*. Milton Keynes, Open University Press.

Lockwood, Fred, and Cooper, Aldwyn, 1980. 'Cicero: Computer-Assisted Learning within an Open University Course'. *Teaching at a Distance*, No. 17.

Loyer, Dennis, 1983. 'Alberta College Hearing Impaired Education Centre PLATO Project'. Edmonton, Alberta College.

Manpower Services Commission, 1983a. 'Towards an Adult Training Strategy: A Discussion Paper'. Sheffield, MSC.

Manpower Services Commission, 1983b. Personal communication from Training Division, Office for Scotland, in letter dated October 10.

Martin, James, 1978. *The Wired Society: A Challenge for Tomorrow*. New Jersey, Prentice-Hall.

Mason, Sir John, 1983. Cited in Anthony Tucker, 'Nations "May Be Ruled by Computer Models" ', *The Scotsman*, August 23.

Matas, Robert, 1983. 'Failed Predictions'. *Globe and Mail, August* 18.

McConnell, D. 1982. 'Cyclops Telewriting Tutorials'. *Teaching at a Distance*, Vol. 22.

McDonald, Shiona, 1983a. 'Community Education Message from Fife'. *Phase Two*, Vol. 3, No. 1.

McDonald, Shiona, 1983b. 'Computers Concerns'. *SCAN*, February.

McDonald, Shiona, 1983c. Personal communication at the Scottish Community Education Microelectronics Project, Glasgow.

McDonald, B., Aitken, R., Jenkins, D., and Kemmis, S. (1977). 'The Educational Evaluation of NDPCAL'. *British Journal of Educational Technology*, Vol. 8, No. 3.

Minsky, Marvin, 1979. 'Computer Science and the Representation of Knowledge'. In Michael Dertouzos and Joel Moses (eds), *The Computer Age: A Twenty Year View*.

Mohr, 1977. Cited in Derek Legge, *The Education of Adults in Britain*.

Morphy, Leslie, 1982. 'The Computer Referral Service'. London, unpublished BBC report.

Noble, 1981, cited in Norman, Colin, *The God that Limps: Science and Technology in the Eighties*.

Norman, Colin, 1981. *The God that Limps: Science and Technology in the Eighties.* London, Norton.

Odor, Phil, 1982. 'Microcomputers and Disabled People'. *International Journal of Man-Machine Studies*, Vol. 17.

OECD, 1982. *The Challenge of Unemployment*. Paris.

Orwell, George, 1954. *Nineteen Eighty-Four*. Harmondsworth, Penguin Books.

O'Shea, Tim, and Self, John, 1983. *Learning and Teaching with Computers*. Brighton, Harvester.

Ottley, Penny, and Kempson, Elaine, 1982. 'Computer Benefits?'. London, National Consumer Council.

Paine, Nigel, 1983. 'Information Technology and Open Learning: The Interactivity Analogue'. Paper presented to ETIC, Exeter, March 28–31. Glasgow, Scottish Council for Educational Technology.

Papert, Seymour, 1980. *Mindstorms: Children, Computers and Powerful Ideas*. Brighton, Harvester Press.

Perkins, W. J. (ed.), 1983. *High Technology Aids for the Disabled*. London, Butterworth.

Prenis, John, 1981. *The Language of Computers*. London, W. H. Allen.

Radcliffe, John, 1983a. Personal communication at the BBC, London.

Radcliffe, John, 1983b. 'BBC Computer Literacy Project Progress Report, June 1983'. London, unpublished BBC report.

Radcliffe, John, and Salkeld, Roberts, 1983. *Towards Computer Literacy: The BBC Computer Literacy Project 1979–1983*. London, BBC Publications.

Reynolds, Angus, 1983. An Introduction to Computer-Based Learning'. *Training and Development Journal*, May.

Roberts, Nancy, and Andersen, David, 1983. *Introduction to Computer Simulation: The System Dynamics Approach*. Reading, Mass., Addison Wesley.

Rogers, Rick, 1983. 'Pick a Winning Combination'. *The Guardian*, August 16.

Ross, P. M., 1980. 'Computers in Education'. Edinburgh: Department of Artificial Intelligence, University of Edinburgh Occasional Paper No. 17.

Rothschild, Joan (ed.), 1982. *Women, Technology and Innovation*. Oxford, Pergamon Press.

Rushby, Nicholas, 1979. *An Introduction to Educational Computing*. London, Croom Helm.

Rushby, Nick (ed.), 1981. *Selected Readings in Computer-based Learning*. London, Kogan Page.

Sage, Morley, and Smith, David, 1983. 'Microcomputers in Education: A Framework for Research'. London, Social Science Research Council.

Salkeld, Roberts, 1983. Personal communication at the BBC, London.

Scanlon, Eileen, Jones, Ann, O'Shea, Tim, Murphy, Pat, Whitelegg, Elizabeth and Vincent, Tom, 1982. 'Computer Assisted Learning'. Milton Keynes, Open University (Institutional Research Review, No. 1).

Scarrot, Gordon, 1981, cited in Butler, David, *Britain and the Information Society*.

SCEMP, 1982a. 'Computers for All: Report on Work in Progress'. Edinburgh, Scottish Council for Community Education.

SCEMP, 1982b. 'Computers for All: Report on Work in Progress'. 2nd ed. Glasgow, Scottish Community Education Microelectronics Project.

SCEMP, 1982c. 'Guidelines for the Design of Computer Programs for Community Use'. Glasgow: Scottish Microelectronics Development Programme.

SCEMP, 1983. 'Report on Work in Progress', 3rd ed. Glasgow, Scottish Community Education Microelectronics Project.

SCET, 1983 'Open Learning Statistics'. Paper for the Scottish Committee on Open Learning'. Glasgow, Scottish Council for Educational Technology.

Scotsman, The, 1983. 'FBI Inquiry into Computer Bank Raids', August 13.

Scriven, 1981. Cited in David Hawkridge, *New Information Technology in Education*.

Sharples, Mike, 1982a. 'Educational Technology and the Open University'. *Teaching at a Distance*, Vol. 22.

Sharples, Mike, 1982b. 'An Evaluation of the Cyclops Telewriting System for Distance Tutoring of Open University Students'. Paper presented to the Conference on Teleconferencing and Interactive Media. University of Wisconsin.

Sharples, Mike and McConnell, David, n.d. 'Distance Teaching by Cyclops: An Educational Evaluation of the Open University's Telewriting System'. Milton Keynes, Institute of Educational Technology, Paper No. 202.

Sheffield Computers for People, 1983. 'Computer Benefit Systems'. *Community Computing Network Newsletter*, No. 2.

Shubik, Martin, 1979, 'Computers and Modeling'. In Michael Dertouzos and Joel Moses (eds), *The Computer Age: A Twenty Year View*.

Sieghart, Paul (ed.), 1982. *Micro-chips wih Everything: The Consequences of Information Technology*. London, Comedia Publishing Group in association with the Institute of Contemporary Arts.

Skues, Nicky, 1983. 'New Horizons', *The Times Educational Supplement*, May 27.

Smith, Keith, 1983. 'Your Back-up'. *See 4*, No. 4.

Smith, Robert, 1983. *Learning How To Learn: Applied Theory for Adults*. Milton Keynes, Open University Press.

Taylor, John, 1983. 'Microtechnology and the Education of Adults'. First draft of the paper by this name published by ACACE.

Toffler, A., 1981. Cited in Mike Sharples, 'Educational Technology and the Open University'.

Tough, Allen, 1971. *The Adult's Learning Projects: A Fresh Approach in Theory and Practice to Adult Learning*. Toronto, Ontario Institute for Studies in Education.

Trudel, Lina, and Belanger, Paul, 1982. 'Computerization: For Better and for Worse'. Montreal, Institut Canadien d'Education des Adultes (paper prepared for the International Council of Adult Education Conference, Paris, October 1982).

Turney, Jon, and Jones, Felicity, 1983. 'The Computer as a Teacher'. *The Times Higher Education Supplement*, April 29.

Vincent, Tom, 1983. 'Home Computing for the Visually Handicapped'. *Teaching at a Distance*, No. 23.

Weizenbaum, Joseph, 1966. Cited in Margaret Boden, *Artificial Intelligence and Natural Man*.

Weizenbaum, Joseph, 1976. *Computer Power and Human Reason*. San Francisco, Freeman.

Weizenbaum, Joseph, 1979. 'Once More: The Computer Revolution'. In Michael Dertouzos and Joel Moses (eds), *The Computer Age: A Twenty Year View*.

Weizenbaum, Joseph, 1982. Cited in Davy, 'The Man in the Belly of the Beast', *The Observer*, August 15.

Werneke, Diane, 1983. *Microelectronics and Office Jobs: The Impact of the Chip on Women's Employment*. Geneva, International Labour Office.

Williams, Shirley, 1982. 'Outlook Boom: Reality or Myth?' In Paul Sieghart (ed.), *Micro-chips with Everything: The Consequences of Information Technology*.

Wilson, Valerie, 1983. 'Computerised Occupational Guidance for Adults: A Case Study'. *Scottish Journal of Adult Education*, Vol. 6, No. 1.

Yanz, Linda, and McCoy, Liza, 1983. 'Microtechnology: An International Conference'. *Participatory Research Newsletter*, No. 2.

Index